WINE
AND
WINE
COOKING

WINE AND WINE COOKING

Entertaining and Cooking with American Wines

BY ANNE M. LOGAN

ARCO
New York

Designed and Illustrated by T. F. Hale

Published 1974 by Arco Publishing Company, Inc.
219 Park Avenue South, New York, N.Y. 10003
by arrangement with Westover Publishing Co.

Copyright © 1972 by Westover Publishing Co.

Library of Congress Catalog Card Number 73-88651
ISBN 0-668-03347-9

Printed in the United States of America

TABLE OF CONTENTS

Acknowledgements

Writing a book is hard work, I discovered. But I also
discovered that many people are generous beyond
belief. I must thank, in particular, Marjorie Lumm
of the Wine Institute's Home Advisory Service for
the excellent recipes she shared with me . . . Shirley,
Jeanne and Laurie Logan who *made* me relax. . . .
and Catherine T. Pendergast and Betty White who
taught me my favorite recipes. And finally,
I'd like to express my gratitude to a friend named
Clyde for patience and fortitude above and beyond. . . .

To my brothers, Jack, Mark and Gerard
and their families.
To my dad, John J. Logan.
And in loving memory of my mother, Anne.

Introduction

As with, I suspect, many Americans, my first meaningful introduction to wine took place in the *boîtes, bistros,* and *cafés* of Paris, the *trattorias* of Rome. Wine was part of the *prix fixe déjeuner* or *diner* and the only decision required was whether one wanted *rouge ou blanc.* The waiter naturally assumed you would have wine – and, however abstemious your upbringing, you wouldn't dream of disillusioning him.

The waiter's illusions remained quite intact – and I acquired a taste for wine. It can be an expensive taste, as I learned upon returning from my twenty-one day excursion! (It can also not be expensive, as I learned later.) Knowing nothing about wine except that I liked it, I was properly awed by maitre d's, wine stewards, and waiters. A disdainful look from a busboy was enough to drive me into throes of humiliation. I finally decided that the only way to ward off the throes was to learn my subject.

I didn't walk, I ran to the public library, which fortunately had a good selection of books by wine experts. The first few I flipped through were obviously above my head (I now flip through them with unseemly smugness!). But finally I discovered several volumes I have cherished ever since. Their authors were among the few who could resist the poesy which attaches itself to most discussions of wine – the rhapsodic comments, the metaphors – and talk about wine in practical terms: how to choose good wine without going broke, how to determine the qualities of aroma, body, taste. Perhaps you're thinking that I, too, have fallen victim to the poetics

1

of wine talk. But certain of these words, however fanciful, are sound descriptions – as you will discover when you discover the wonderful world of wine. Despite its title, this book is intended to be about *all* wine. However, Americans have developed an inferiority complex about such arts as eating and drinking, so long regarded as the exclusive pleasures of our European brothers. Americans believe they suffer from the "meat and potatoes" syndrome even though they occasionally savor *Wiener Schnitzel, Hungarian Goulash, Potato Kügel,* and *Swedish Meatballs.* These dishes, after all, are good, sturdy, homely fare; that they are also part of the world's grande cuisine hardly impresses most Americans.

The same is true of American wines – and it might well be true of many more products of Americana. Even the American who accepts wine as a part of entertaining is usually not secure enough to serve his guests a homegrown vintage. Instead he presents the impressively labelled imports! Only if the host is caught short is an American wine likely to be admitted to the party, and even then, its presence becomes the subject of an apology!

Here are described some of the world's great wines. Unfortunately, they are reasonably priced, which immediately makes them suspect. And they are domestic! As to that, H. G. Wells commented: "You Americans have the loveliest wines in the world, you know, but you don't realize it. You call them domestic, and that's enough to cause trouble anywhere." Hopefully this book will dispel America's timidity about wine – particularly its own.

3

THE STORY OF WINE

"Where there is no wine, there is no love"
— *Euripides*

Wine is probably the oldest beverage known to
man — except, of course, water. It is guessed that as
early as the Stone Age — over 5000 years ago —
ancient man began cultivating grapes for food, and
not much later he discovered that the juice of
fermented grapes was good to drink.

The earliest vineyards appeared in Asia Minor, in
what today is Iran. This was the original home of
the *Vitis vinifera*, the grape species which traveled
on Phoenician ships first to the Mediterranean
countries of Europe, and many centuries later, on
Spanish ships to the New World.

Since Iran was the first vineyard country, it is not
surprising that the legend of the "discovery" of wine
concerns a lovely Persian lady — a lovelorn lady in
the harem of the king. She felt that she had lost her
place as his favorite and decided to kill herself.

Now it happened that the king was very fond of
grapes — so fond that he stored them in large jars,
enabling him to enjoy them the year 'round. But,
one day, he tasted from a jar of bitter grapes and
ordered the jar to be labelled Poison. (He could have
just thrown them out, but that would have ruined
the story.) Naturally, this was the jar his neglected
lady discovered. She poured out some of the liquid
and drank deeply; but instead of death, she found
her depression gone. In fact, she felt almost happy.
She certainly no longer wished to die. Thereafter,

5

whenever a dark mood came over her — i.e. when the king was too attentive to one of his other ladies — she would pour a glass of her secret "poison" and drink it. Invariably, her spirits would soar. Soon, she had regained the sparkling gaiety which originally had captivated the king — and, of course, he fell in love with her all over again! Their happiness restored, the lady told her master about her attempt at suicide and the strange effects of her special "poison." Upon investigation, the king discovered that the grapes in that jar had been damaged; their skins were broken and many of them had been crushed. For months, they had lain in the dark storeroom, their juice turning (or fermenting) into wine.

From that time, the king ordered a certain portion of each grape crop to be crushed and laid away so that the juice might turn into the magical beverage which had restored his lady's lively spirits. The two of them lived happily ever after of course — and, of course, drinking wine.

A pretty story but more important, it illustrates the basic process of winemaking.

Even without the help of the romantic Persians, there is little doubt that wine would have taken its place among the gifts of nature most prized by mankind. There are references to wine in the hieroglyphics of ancient Egypt as well as in Chinese literature dating back to 2000 B.C. The Bible contains countless mentions of wine. In Judaism it is ranked with bread as a heavenly gift for which a special prayer of thanksgiving must be said. And when archaeologists unearthed the ruins of the ancient city of Gideon near Jerusalem, they found the ruins of a huge commercial winery, including the stone presses in which the grapes were crushed. In the New Testament, wine is the result of Christ's first recorded miracle — at the Marriage of Cana — and it is wine which, in the Catholic Mass, is transformed into Christ's blood.

Around the sixth century B.C., the seafaring Phoenicians introduced wine grapes into Europe, more specifically, to Greece, where the beverage drunk by Plato and Aristotle was flavored with resin, and was the forerunner of today's popular Greek

retsina. (Socrates added hemlock, which produced
an entirely different kind of drink, but he was under
considerable pressure to find a quick way out.) The
Greeks so highly prized wine that they attributed it
to Divine Providence and assigned it a patron,
Dionysus.

With the rise of the Roman Empire, Dionysus
became Bacchus, and after Caesar's conquest of Gaul,
vineyards had sprung up throughout southern
Europe. By the fifth century A.D., Europe had
become the wine center of the world. In the years
500 to 1400, churchmen added winemaking to the
arts they were to keep alive during the Dark Ages,
and it was in the monasteries that many of the
refinements of viticulture and oenology were
developed. The monks became the winemakers of
Europe.

(It is interesting that the wine industry of America
is also in debt to the Catholic Church; the early
plantings by the missionary priests in California, for
example — and two of the country's oldest and most
famous vineyards were founded by religious orders —
the Brotherhood Vineyard of New York and The
Christian Brothers of Mont La Salle in the Napa
Valley of California.)

Eventually, the great vineyards of Europe emerged —
in France, Germany, Italy, Switzerland, Portugal,
and Spain.

8

Wine in America

When Lief Erikson's Viking ships hove to off the
coast of North America, the sailors gazed in wonder
at the luxuriant vines, heavily laden with clusters of
grapes, which seemed to blanket the shore. The
name for this new world came quite naturally —
Vinland, a land of vines. Fortunately, Erikson's
sailors hadn't the time to try to make wine from the
grapes — they ate a few and found them tasty. But
there's a far difference between the grape and the
wine!

The grapes native to North America were cousin to
the *Vitis vinifera* of Europe. Over milleniums of
adjustment to the often violent climates of the

Eastern seaboard, these *Vitis labrusca* and *Vitis riparia* vines had developed a hardiness and a definitely hardy flavor which produced a wine very different from the delicate *vinifera* that had led such a sheltered life in the valleys and hillsides of Europe.

The first settlers in America were equally enthusiastic about the luxurious vines — until they tried to make wine from the grapes. The beverage, while drinkable, did not at all suit the taste of our forefathers whose palates had been conditioned by the classic *vinifera* wines of Europe. Of course, in those early days, winemaking took second place to the matter of survival, so it was not until the mid-1700s that prosperous landowners began importing vines from Europe for planting in the New World. Among them was Thomas Jefferson. But even he did not foresee the hazards of transplanting a veritable hothouse flower to what was a wilderness. The *vinifera* vines died during the first winter, and for those who could afford it, wine remained one of the old-country products with which America could not quite sever its ties.

However, unknown to Jefferson and his fellow would-be viticulturists, the prized *vinifera* vines were taking hold in California. They were planted by the humble Franciscan monks who had followed the conquistadors from Spain to Mexico, and had traveled North, following the coastline, building missions and ministering to the Indians. A young

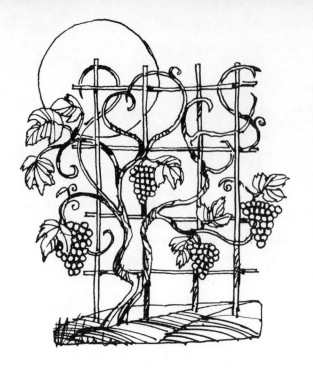

padre, Junipero Serra, is generally credited as the
first person to plant these grapes, at Mission San
Angelo (near what is now San Diego) in 1769. The
monks' objective was to obtain enough wine for use
on the altar. The mission grapes fulfilled their need.
However, though a vast improvement over any wine
previously produced in this country, the bluish-black
mission grapes yielded a wine that was but a hint
of the fine, even great vintages to come.

The Founding Fathers of California's Wine Industry

In 1833 Jean Louis Vignes, a young winemaker
from Bordeaux, settled upon a plot of land near what
is now Los Angeles and began planting vine cuttings
he had brought with him from France. Other than
the mission grapes, these were the first varieties of
vinifera to be grown in the New World, and the
wines Vignes made were the finest yet produced in
America. It was a beginning.

The next illustrious name in the industry belonged
to a young Mexican officer, General Vallejo, who, as
commander of the California army ruled over the
vast territory which encompassed Napa and Sonoma
counties. He took over many of the old mission
vineyards around the town of Sonoma, where he made
his home, and replanted them with new European
cuttings. By 1841 he was producing small quantities
of excellent wine. After obtaining from his government grants of thousands of acres of land in the
same area, he expanded his production, but never
allowed his standards of quality to slip. His red
wines, and particularly his clarets, were especially
notable.

When the people of California finally broke away
from Mexico and formed a Republic in 1846, Vallejo
was jailed. But for some reason his property was not
confiscated, and, after his release a short time later,
he returned to his winery and winemaking.

"Count" Haraszthy

The stories about Agoston Haraszthy are legion. In
what seems to be the reliable one, he was the eldest
son of a wealthy Hungarian family who rashly took
part in an abortive anti-Austrian revolution. With
his wife and several children, he managed to escape
the Emperor's wrath and made his way to America,
arriving in New York about 1840. Always more than
a bit of a wheeler-dealer, he was able to provide
for his family and transport them first to the
Midwest and finally to California, where they arrived
precisely in midst of the Gold Rush. But the

Count's* experienced eye saw another kind of gold in the hills and valleys. He recognized immediately that this was wine country, and managed to convince the Governor of California to grant him a commission to travel the vineyards of Europe in search of vine cuttings. He left for the Old World in 1861, on the eve of the Civil War, and returned a year later to find the country in the midst of that tragic confrontation and the state of California neither in the mood or with the money to pay for his expedition and the cuttings he had collected. For once the fox was outfoxed, but the state benefited; Haraszthy's vines were taken by individual planters who carefully matched them to California's many "micro-climates" — from the cool mountains of the north to the warm, sun-drenched southern valleys — duplicates of virtually every one of the great winegrowing regions of Europe.

It is estimated that Haraszthy brought back from Europe over 100,000 cuttings of about three hundred grape varieties. And since these cuttings, planted throughout the state, were the forebears of today's California vineyards, it is perhaps not unjust that the controversial Count is the frontrunner for the title of "father" of the industry.

---

*Recognizing a certain reverence among the democratic Americans for a title, however spurious, Haraszthy adopted the title "Count." Later, upon moving westward, he was to discover that the less sophisticated pioneer stock had little regard for such distinctions, and he switched to the more manly sounding "Colonel," which for Haraszthy had about as much validity as "Count." In California, however, he decided to rejoin royalty, built himself a palatial home only slightly less grand than the Parthenon, and resumed the title "Count."

14

Haraszthy never lived to see his dream of an American wineland realized. Always ready for a new adventure (and possibly a new and larger fortune), he set out on a Central American journey that should have led to lost treasures. Instead, it led to a watery end when the Count lost his grip while swinging Tarzan-style across a Nicaraguan river. The crocodiles waited below.

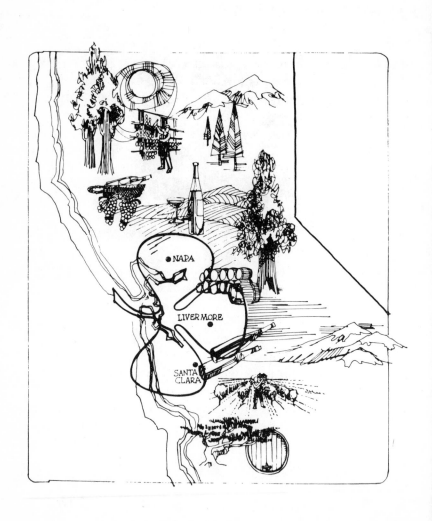

AMERICA'S WINELANDS

"Wine is a constant proof that God loves us and loves to see us happy."

— Benjamin Franklin

California Vineyards

If you were to take a map of California and draw a 3-leaf clover with its center at San Francisco and one leaf extending north to Asti, one east through the Livermore Valley, and another south through San Jose, you would have a handy diagram of the great winegrowing districts of the state: the Napa Valley to the north, the wide lowland expanse of Livermore, the mountains-plains complex of Santa Clara-San Benito.

California is literally dotted with wineries, large and small. However, only a small percentage are known outside of the state, and even fewer nationwide.

The Napa Valley

Buena Vista   It might be said that this is where it all began, for Buena Vista was founded by Count Agoston Haraszthy. Known officially as Haraszthy Cellars-Buena Vista, the winery is located just outside the sleepy little town of Sonoma on Old Winery Road. Since it has been declared an historic landmark, there are numerous signs to direct you. The old road winds under a canopy of trees that filter the sunlight, reminiscent of the proverbial enchanted forest. Finally you come to the courtyard of the original winery, gray stoned, vine covered. A series of arrows guide you through the winery and aging cellars, with photographs depicting its history, including the 1906 earthquake which devastated not only Buena Vista, but most of the vineyards in the state.

Not far from the winery is the site of Haraszthy's home. No longer standing, it has become a legend in every sense of the word since it was a palatial Greek-style mansion with neo-Classic statues perched every few feet along the roof's edge. A monument to vanity and bad taste, it must have been considered the greatest of palaces by the immigrant Italian and French winemakers who were struggling to set up the very basics of their livelihoods, to say nothing of its effect on the Chinese laborers. But Haraszthy was a man who lived in the grandest style even when his finances were at their lowest.

Buena Vista is still very productive today, producing exceptional wines including the rare Green Hungarian — a tart, dry white wine of distinctive flavor and bouquet, as well as appetizer and dessert wines of high quality.

Charles Krug   Russian-born Charles Krug was one of the pioneers in California wine. He established his St. Helena winery in 1861, producing the superb wines that made his name a synonym for excellence. Although the winery changed hands several times after Krug's death, the value of the name continued. The present owners — the Mondavis — Cesare Mondavi's widow, Rosa, and his son Peter have kept the Krug name. (Another son, Robert, has established his own notable winery a few miles down the road.)

Charles Krug winery has a special VIP tasting room which is a treat to view even from the outside. It's a turn-of-the-century Union Pacific railroad car, which sits on the tracks of a now-unused railroad siding. It is replete with a semi-circular oak bar and leather-covered banquette seats and tables. Inside, one feels as though he has stepped back into another, more graceful era, and the view from the windows of the vineyards and mountains, unmarred by any modern structure, reinforces the illusion. Named "Rosa," for his wife the car provides a rather endearing insight into the sentiments of the late Cesare Mondavi.

Inglenook A long, slender stretch of land framed by low, rolling mountains, the Napa Valley is perhaps the most beautiful of all the California winelands. Highway 29 runs directly down through its center, and on either side of the road the vineyards stretch into the distance. Because the valley is so narrow, it is easy to spot the wineries nestled in the foothills of the mountains.

One of the loveliest is Inglenook, a gray-stoned, vine-covered building built right at the hillside. The cellars, tunneled deep into the hill when the winery was built, are still in use, their cool, steady temperature providing the best climate for aging the wines.

The story of Inglenook is most colorful. It was founded in the 1860s by Gustave Ferdinand Nybom, a Finnish sea captain who had made a fortune in the Alaskan fur trade. His avocation was oenology, and when he retired from the sea, he made it his vocation. Almost single-handedly he built Inglenook into one of the most important premium wineries. (Although Inglenook is now owned by United Vintners, whose holdings also include one of the giants of the industry, Italian Swiss Colony, the quality of its wines remains superb. Huge companies are increasingly acquiring smaller firms for better marketing, but the new owners have wisely refrained from interfering in the making of the wines, knowing this could destroy the reputation of the brand. At Inglenook, as at many other wineries, the original winemakers are still in charge of making the wine.)

One of the most interesting features of a tour at Inglenook is the special tasting room built by Captain Nybom. An exact duplicate of his own dining room aboard his old sailing ship, it is decorated with bottle glass, carved wood paneling, antique cups, wine glasses, and decanters.

Italian Swiss Colony   About eighty-five miles north of San Francisco on Highway 101, colorful signs invite you to the Italian Swiss Colony winery at Asti. It is not to be missed!

Founded by Italian financier Andrea Sbarboro in 1881, Asti (also the name of a famed winemaking town in Italy) became a mecca for immigrant Italian and Swiss vintners.

Originally Sbarboro had planned the winery as a cooperative, with the workers building up equity in the company. But the immigrants preferred to be

20

employees because they liked regular wages coming in, and so Italian Swiss remained a private concern. Nevertheless, the spirit of the original winemakers is still in evidence, not only in the wide variety of wines, ranging from Italian-style Chianti to classic Grenache Rosé, but in the tasting rooms, where waiters and waitresses in colorful national costumes serve you samples of their delicious wines.

A unique feature at Italian Swiss is the old chapel of Our Lady of Carmel, built in the shape of a giant wine cask. Though, since the erection of the new modern church next door, it is no longer in use, it still stands, a testament to the simple faith of those early settlers.

Hanns Kornell Champagne Cellars   Hanns Kornell arrived in America in the late 1930s, penniless, but with one treasure—the winemaking knowledge of generations of German Champagne makers. He made his way to California, where, with the help of other winemakers, he started his own small vineyard. Today he is still small, but in a big way. Hanns Kornell is perhaps the best Champagne made in the United States—and possibly anywhere. While Kornell does make other wines, he concentrates on Champagne, which is made in the classic way, and marketed as Hanns Kornell Third Generation Champagne.

Louis M. Martini   Surely one of the most famous of the California wineries is this proud home of some of the very best wines produced in America. Any visit to the Napa Valley must include the

Louis M. Martini winery – along with a tasting of the excellent red wines in particular. Especially not to be missed is this vineyard's superb Mountain Zinfandel.

A good illustration of the very personal interest and devotion of winemakers is an anecdote about the fiery, temperamental Louis M. Martini, Founding Father of the firm. At one very gala charity affair attended by San Francisco society, there was to be a special wine tasting. As usual, Martini arrived early and meticulously went around examining the tables, checking the temperature of the wines, sniffing the glasses – the standard precautions taken by wine experts. He picked up a glass and immediately his sensitive nose told him something was wrong. The waiter confirmed that the glasses had been washed in detergent rather than soap – a cardinal sin, since detergent leaves an undesirable taste in the glass which can affect the wine. Martini was outraged, and ordered the waiter to rinse the glasses in boiling water.

The waiter coolly replied that he was not paid to wash glasses. Undaunted, Martini looked around, spotted some of the arriving ladies – resplendent in satins and silks, dripping with jewels – and commandeered them into the kitchen to rinse the offending glassware.

An amusing story, and one which demonstrates to what extremes a winemaker will go to protect his wine.

22

The Livermore Valley

Unlike Napa, the Livermore Valley is a wide, almost
bowl-like flatland with low mountains ringing it in
the distance. The gravelly soil is particularly good
for white wines, although some spectacular reds
are produced there as well. It is a particularly serene
valley, with little in the way of tourist attractions.
No road signs mar the view of the vineyards. The
roads cross at right angles and the towns are small,
often only a few blocks square. It seems one of the
most peaceful spots on earth.

Wente Bros.   While most wineries have excellent
facilities for visitors – guided tours, tasting rooms,
picnic grounds – it is unfortunate that tourists seldom
have the opportunity of meeting the vintners themselves. I was privileged to meet some of them and I
came away, not only knowing more about wine, but
with new insight into the very personal business
winemaking really is.

Karl Wente, of the famed Wente Bros. winery,
greeted us in khakis and canvas boots spotted with
mud. I was doubtful, but soon learned that the mud
was genuine, the result of tramping through the
vineyards supervising the harvest, just as his father
and grandfather had done. Karl Wente spoke of
his wines with quiet pride that just managed to
disguise his enthusiasm. And he certainly is
entitled to be enthusiastic. Wente Bros. wines –
particularly their excellent whites – have earned
recognition and applause from discerning wine lovers
the world over.

Concannon Vineyard   Lest it be thought that the
French, Germans, and Italians have a monopoly on
fine winemaking, we toast one James Concannon of
County Galway, Ireland. After arriving in this
country – and after a number of business ventures in
less rewarding fields – James settled down to viticulture. At the urging of his local priest, he first
concentrated on sacramental wines for the Mass –
an area which is still dominated by the Concannon
family. Along the way, however, Concannon began
planting vines which would eventually produce
extraordinary table wines, both red and white.
It is one of the few wineries which markets Petite
Sirah, a rich, hearty red which originated in the
Rhone Valley. Hard to get, because wine-wise
customers buy up all they can find, Concannon
wines are among the best America has to offer.

Incidentally, the winery is still as Irish as when it
was born: Concannon's sons and grandsons have
taken to wine as if they'd never heard of ale. And
the origin of the winery has not been forgotten:
Concannon is still one of the primary suppliers of
sacramental wine for churches.

Santa Clara-San Benito

South of San Francisco, Highway 101 brings you to
the Santa Clara-San Benito district, a vast
mountain-plains complex which is the home of some
of California's finest wineries.

24

Almadén   One of the best-known California brands,
Almadén was founded by Bordeaux winemaker
Etienne Thée, who, like so many Californians,
arrived during the Gold Rush. He may have intended
to make his fortune in gold, but wine was in his
destiny. He purchased an old winery in Los Gatos
and took as his partner a compatriot, Charles LeFranc.

LeFranc later graduated from partner to heir-apparent when he married Thée's daughter, Adele. And he did well by both wife and wine. Under his management, Almadén became the largest winery in California by the 1880s.

Almadén is noted not only for some fine varietals — especially its Pinot Noir and Grenache Rosé — but also for its red and white Burgundies, named Mountain Red and White, which come in decorative, distinctively shaped jugs that many people like to re-use as planters and vases. However, the popularity of Almadén wines is based on their quality — not their containers.

Paul Masson Paul Masson, a Frenchman descended from a Burgundy family, joined the winery founded by Thée, soon to become known as LeFranc-Masson. Following his partner's example, Masson married the LeFranc daughter and eventually established his own winery high in the rolling hills above Saratoga.

Many wine novices think that Paul Masson is a French wine, which is not so strange since Masson is well known in Europe, the pioneer exporter of American wines.

From the very beginning, Paul Masson exhibited not only a fine knowledge of oenology but of publicity as well. Every notable to visit San Francisco — and in the last decades of the nineteenth century many luminaries of stage, opera, and the literary world wended their ways west — was presented with Paul

26

Masson Champagne. Not the least of the celebrities to be so honored was the musical star Anna Held, whose famed bath in Paul Masson Champagne was headline material for the nation's press. From the note of appreciation Miss Held wrote to Paul Masson, it may be assumed that she drank some of it as well.

One of the most delightful aspects of visiting the Paul Masson vineyards is "Music in the Vineyards," a summer-long series of concerts and light opera performed on the stone patio in front of the old winery, now no longer in use. The building is set in a hollow, the hillside rising around to form an outdoor amphitheater. The audience sits in chairs, protected from the afternoon sun by parasols, or along the hillside on picnic blankets. At intermission they are fêted with Paul Masson Champagne, of course. It makes for an idyllic afternoon and shouldn't be missed by anyone planning a trip to Northern California.

Mirrasou Vineyards Further south, at Soledad, is another fine winery and one that is becoming increasingly known all over the country. Mirrasou was founded in the mid-1880s by Pierre Pellier. As with Almadén, the marriage of Pellier's daughter changed both the name and character of the winery, and Pellier's grandsons, Edmund and Norbert Mirrasou, concentrated on the production of varietal wines for sale to other wineries for use in blending.

27

But *their* sons had different ideas. The five Mirrasou boys wanted to market their wines under the family name—and with vintage dates! The fathers succumbed to the youthful enthusiasm, with the result that the Mirrasou label has taken its place among the most distinguished brands in the country.

Mirrasou produces some outstanding white wines, notably a fine Gewurztraminer and a Chenin Blanc. It is also one of the few producers of Petite Sirah. On our visit we were also privileged to taste a new wine made, so far, only by Mirrasou: Petite Rosé, a fruity, tangy fresh wine with an exquisite rose color. Steve Mirrasou explained that Petite Rosé was the result of a fortuitous mistake. It seems that a carload of Petite Sirah grapes had been brought in, pressed, and the juice drawn off after a few hours, as in the making of rosé. After the error was discovered, it was decided to let the wine go through fermentation, just to see what would happen. What happened was Petite Rosé, which we predict will become an outstanding favorite once it is marketed in quantity.

In no way can this be considered a comprehensive list of California wineries. It actually represents some of the few we visited. The names of several others may be familiar: Beaulieu Vineyards, whose Cabernet Sauvignon cannot be surpassed; Sebastiani, founded by the Franciscan monks and one of the oldest, most honored in the state; Schramsberg in Napa, noted for its superb Champagnes; Guild Wine

Company in Lodi, a giant of the industry and producer of excellent popularly priced table wines as well as appetizer and dessert wines; Heitz Cellars, a small winery which produces fine table wines that are hard to find but worth the search; the renowned Christian Brothers winery at Mt. La Salle, whose cellars of premium and popular wines in all categories are presided over by Brother Timothy, and are surely among the best known American wines; and Gallo, the vast winery built by the brothers Ernest and Julio who have been pioneers in the development of new and better winemaking techniques (usually in cooperation with the University of California School of Viticulture and Oenology) and whose brand is perhaps the best recognized of any wine served in the United States.

Winemaking in the Eastern United States

At one time, native American grapes grew wild across the United States, from the East Coast to the Rockies. They made poor wine. But eventually they were tamed by careful selection and cross-breeding, resulting in varieties with such names as Concord, Delaware, Catawba, Dutchess, Elvira, Fredonia, Isabella, Clinton, Missouri Riesling and Niagara. The wines these grapes yield, whether red or white, are all distinguished by the special American grape flavor, and while some refer to this taste as "foxy," it is perhaps more accurate to describe it as highly flavored and fruity, for the fruit flavor is quite dominant.

While wine is produced in several of the eastern
states, New York State—which ranks next to
California in United States production—must be
considered the wineland of the East. Its principal
wine regions are the Finger Lakes, the areas
bordering on Lake Erie, and parts of the Hudson
Valley.

The Finger Lakes district, with its deep, narrow blue
lakes and its steep hillsides is the most famous and
the founding father was the Reverend William
Bustwick, an Episcopal minister in Hammondsport,
New York—still the wine center of the East, just
as Napa is in the West. In his rectory garden,
planted with young vine cuttings, the good Reverend
unwittingly founded a multi-million dollar industry,
for his neighbors followed suit and soon were
producing bountiful harvests that were the forebears
of today's crops.

True, the vines they grew were of the *vitis labrusca*
variety and the wines had the customary grape
flavor. But by this time—the mid-eighteenth century
—Americans, except for the wealthy few, had lost
their taste for wine as it was known in Europe. The
homegrown variety seemed perfectly fine. At the
same time, a strong temperance movement was
growing in the land. Wine was the only respectable
beverage around and, predictably, it prospered.

Today, eastern wine has evolved into a far more
sophisticated beverage: crossbreeding with European
stock and interbreeding with other *labrusca* vines
has resulted in a wide range of interesting varietals.

30

Boordy Perhaps the most important development in wine making in the East began several decades ago when Philip Wagner of Maryland, who dabbled in viticulture as a hobby, suddenly became interested in French experiments in cross-breeding native American vines with European *Vitis vinifera* thereby producing new grape varieties with the fruit qualities of the best European strains and the hardiness of most American species. Wagner, whose own small vineyard was named Boordy — a name destined to become famous in the language of wine — exhaustively tested his own vines, interbreeding European and American vines to develop a vine with the best qualities of both. And in fact, the vines he grew did inherit the resistance to cold and disease of their American ancestors, while retaining the fine qualities of the European vines.

Wagner wrote volumes on the subject of his hybrids, and more important, he distributed his vines to other sections of the country for further testing and planting in commercial vineyards. As of now, extensive vineyards in New York State, Ohio, Maryland, and Pennsylvania are thriving from Wagner cuttings and show every promise of yielding high quality wines.

Following Wagner's experiments at Boordy (and the Boordy Vineyards are now prospering in New York State as well as Maryland) other vintners began their own experiments. The vines they have produced bear names and numbers unfamiliar to the wine drinking public, mainly because they are principally used for blending. It is highly unlikely that you will ever come across a Baco #1 or a Seibel #10878. However, these grapes play an enormously important part in winemaking east of the Rockies just as Boordy Vineyard's Philip Wagner played a vital role in the development of winemaking in the East. Perhaps the best testament to his genius is his wine. Hard to find, it is nonetheless well worth the effort.

Vinifera Vineyards   Another pioneer in the development of eastern vineyards is Dr. Konstantin Frank, a German emigré whose winemaking family had faced similar hardships of climate while trying to cultivate *vinifera* vineyards in Russia at the request of the Soviet government.

Upon studying the American vines and their Europeanized offshoots, Dr. Frank recognized that any vines grown in the East would have to be bred to ripen early because of the relatively short growing season . . . and, of course they would have to be hardy enough to withstand the freezing winters. After years of experimentation, Dr. Frank succeeded in what is virtually a miracle—he has grown the great grape varieties of Germany and France and made exquisite wines from them—Chardonnays, Rieslings and Pinot Noirs.

However, the production of Vinifera Vineyards is necessarily limited by the extraordinary care which must be lavished on the vines, with the result that Dr. Frank's wines are difficult to come by and expensive when they are available. But should you ever come across a bottle, it is certainly worth the investment.

Taylor Wine Company   Perhaps the best known of the New York wineries is Taylor, founded in 1880 by Walter and Addie Taylor. Walter was a cooper — he manufactured wooden containers, including wine barrels. Drawn to the Finger Lakes by the prospering wine industry, he bought a small vineyard on Lake Keuka near Hammondsport. Before long, he was able to expand this winery to include a large farm — rather prophetically named Bully Hill. Before long, Taylor was producing red and white dinner wines which found a ready market in New York City. Dessert wines followed, but the Champagnes which would eventually become the principals of the Taylor line had to wait until the young winemaker acquired the expensive facilities and special equipment required to make sparkling wine.

In 1962, Taylor Wine Company — which is still owned and operated by the Taylor family — purchased the neighboring Pleasant Valley Wine Company and added the Great Western label to its line. The union of these two companies virtually made Taylor the Gallo of the East.

Their wines cover the range of appetizer, red, white and Rosé, as well as dessert and sparkling wines. They also include such generics as Burgundy and Claret, as well as such proprietary names as Lake Country Red — and White. Among the Champagnes, the most famous remains Great Western.

Widmer Wine Cellars   Probably best known after
Taylor are the Widmer Cellars at Naples on Lake
Canandaigua. Widmer is justifiably famous for its
varietal wines made wholly of the varietal grape
named: Catawba, Lake Niagara, Delaware, Moore's
Diamond. And, unlike most of the eastern wineries,
Widmer dates its vintages: "New York, like Europe,
has years of good and poor vintages."

In addition to its American varietals, Widmer has
been very successful with Riesling and with one of
the French-American hybrids, Seibel Rosé, a
particularly nice pink wine.

However, it is Sherry of which Widmer is especially
proud. Produced without the *flor* yeast which
unfortunately will not develop in the New York
climate, these sherries are aged on the roof of the
winery where they are baked by the sun day in and
out for anywhere from four to eight years. And for
some mysterious reason — wine consistently manages
to elude science — some Widmer sherries are distinctly
Jerez in character!

Gold Seal Vineyards   Bordering on the Taylor-
Great Western vineyards on Lake Keuka is Gold
Seal, which rose to prominence after World War II
under the expert management of Charles Fournier,
formerly the manager of one of France's largest
Champagne companies.

Fournier was keenly interested in Philip Wagner's
experiments with hybrids and Gold Seal wines
benefited from that interest. However, while the

34

company produces generic Rhines, Clarets, Burgundies and Rosés, as well as such varietals as Delaware, Catawba and Pink Catawba, its primary reputation lies with its Champagne. Named for the man who breathed life into Gold Seal, they are called Charles Fournier Champagne, a name many unknowing customers take to be French and are pleasantly amazed when they learn they are drinking a New York State vintage.

Just a note about Champagne: it was discovered that the double fermentation process used in making champagne somehow dissipated the "foxy" flavor of the American grape. Just before the Civil War, the first New York State Champagnes went on the market — and were instantly successful, especially in such metropolises as Boston, New York and Philadelphia. These sparkling wines — the product of vineyards along the shore of Lake Keuka — have contributed largely to the reputation of New York State as "the Champagne region of America."

Pinot Noir Vine

THE VINEYARDS AND THE VINES

"Those lodes and pockets of earth, more precious than the precious ores . . . and the wine is bottled poetry."
—Robert Louis Stevenson

Most important in a successful vineyard is the matching of grape type to environment — soil and weather. While dessert wine grapes thrive in deep soils and warm, sunny climes, dinner wine grapes require cool hillsides.

Different grapes produce different wines and have different characteristics and needs. The fat, sweet grapes which produce Sherries, Madeiras, and Ports — the appetizer and dessert wines — contain a much smaller percentage of acid than the grapes used to make drier table wines. The acid content is determined not only by the grape variety, but by temperature; the higher the temperature the lower the acid content. In dessert wines, which we want to be smooth and mellow as well as sweet, acidity is undesirable. But a table wine without the proper acidity, or tartness, would taste flat.

In a new vineyard, wine grapevines are planted from cuttings — 400 to 600 vines to an acre — and the vintner expects to devote at least four years of continual care and cultivation before his vineyard will yield a full crop. Throughout the life of the vine — on the average about 40 years — constant, loving, year-round attention is essential. In fact, winegrowing requires more detailed and expert supervision than almost any other form of agriculture.

37

The enemies of the vines are many and they are often fatal. At one time, the most dreaded was phylloxera, a root disease that literally ravaged America and Europe in the 1880s, laying to waste the vast, precious vineyards of France, Italy, Germany, and California. Oddly enough, only the *Vitis vinifera* vines were affected. The native American varieties — *Vitis labrusca* and *Vitis riparia* — seemed immune to the root pest.

Science finally came to the rescue with experimental graftings of *vinifera* vines on *labrusca* and *riparia* roots. The result was a phylloxera-resistant vine which may well have saved the wine industry although it required the lengthy process of grafting selected grape varieties on American roots and replanting vast acres of vineyards.

But it worked. And today most California and many European vines are growing on the phylloxera-resistant roots of the hardy native grapevines that so impressed our first settlers.

The Grapes

Wine grapes begin as a cluster of berries on a stem. Pruning controls the number of the clusters on each vine: the fewer clusters, the larger the grapes.

During the first rapid growing period, the amount of sugar in the grape is low. It is only during a long, slow ripening period that the sugar increases to the proper level: for dinner wines about 22 percent.

Dessert wines are allowed to ripen longer, or until the sugar content reaches about 24 percent. Left to ripen too long, however, the grapes may exceed the desired sugar level. Thus the vintage date is critical.

The Harvest

Inspired by colorfully written guidebooks, most people picture the wine harvest as a gay occasion, with happy peasants singing melodies from Sigmund Romberg as they pluck bunches of plump grapes from the vine.

In fact, harvest is one of the most crucial times in the vineyard. Once the winemaker's careful inspection has determined that the grapes are fully ripened, no time is lost. Harvesting is still mainly done by hand with a special scissor or a curved-blade knife. Mechanical harvesting is used only experimentally in some of the flatter vineyard lands of California, and has not yet been employed on an industry-wide basis. It is questionable if the intricate machines will ever prove useful on hillside vineyards.

At one time, the picked grapes were dropped into baskets and carried to wagons which took them to the crushing machines. Today, large metal hoppers designed to fit between the rows of vines travel up and down, picking up the harvest and delivering it to the crushing area much more efficiently than human labor, however picturesque, could accomplish.

The Crush

Before entrance to the crusher — "press," because of its gentler connotation, is the term preferred by vintners — the stems and any leaves are removed from the grape clusters by a machine of unfailing accuracy. The grapes are then dumped into the press, which is a cylindrical, drum-like vehicle with hundreds of perforations.

As the drum revolves at high speed, centrifugal force presses the grapes against the sides, breaking the skins and allowing the juice to ooze out through the holes. While this method may sound less romantic than the ancient practice of trodding the grapes into wine with bare feet, it is certainly more efficient and probably more sanitary.

It is from this first crush that the finest premium wines are made. Some large producers, especially those that ship bulk wines for blending by other winemakers, take advantage of the juice remaining in the grapes — as much as a third of the entire yield. Though not as distinctive as the juice from the first crush, this second crush plays an important part in winemaking all over the world.

Fermentation

Fermentation is the chemical process by which the grape sugars are converted into alcohol and carbon dioxide. While wild yeasts on the skins of grapes will cause the crushed grapes to ferment, most modern winemakers prefer to help nature along by adding a "starter" yeast produced from grape juice.

The length of time the juice is allowed to ferment determines the dryness of the wine. To obtain completely dry dinner wines the juice is allowed to ferment until virtually all of its sugar has been converted. For sweeter table wines, such as a sweet Sauterne, fermentation is halted while a trace of sugar remains. For very sweet dessert wines, the period of fermentation is shortest. To stop the process while there is still a considerable amount of sweetness, wine brandy is added. Thus the term "fortified" to describe these wines.

Red wine grapes are fermented with their skins and seeds for three or four days. The skins release their color (the inner pulp of most grapes is colorless), the seeds their tannin, which gives red wines their desirable astringency. Finally, the juice is "drawn off" the solid matter and allowed to continue fermenting in another container.

The grapes of Rosé wines ferment with their skins and pulp for a shorter time—about twenty to thirty hours—before the juice is drawn off. This accounts for their delicate color and slight astringency.

White wines are fermented without their skins and any differences in color of the wines (which may range from deep gold to palest straw) are attributable to the grapes themselves. Though red wine enthusiasts seem to outnumber the fans of white wine, there are more varieties of white wine, and each has a distinctive characteristic, a different aroma, a different hue.

Fermentation of grapes for even the very driest wines is usually completed within two weeks, after which the wine is drawn off once again, this time to get rid of the pulp and yeast. Other foreign substances are then removed by adding such ingredients as gelatin, which attracts any sediment suspended in the liquid. This clarifying process is repeated several times before the wine is finally bottled. However, because many wines continue to produce sediment during bottle aging, some very old wines must be carefully decanted to prevent the sediment from entering the glass.

Aging

Most of the wines we drink are young—perhaps a year after they are bottled. But there is an aging process before bottling which is all important in the winemaking process.

Wine in bulk is aged in casks—in the case of whites and roses, these "casks" might very well be glass-lined containers specially equipped to handle the very special requirements of fine wine. The long-lived reds are aged in casks of oak or redwood—the wood helping to "marry" the complex elements of the wine. (An indication of the importance of wood for aging these wines is the use by some vintners of relatively small, oval casks—because the oval shape allows the wine more contact with the wood.)

While even the fullest bodied whites do not require more than a year in wood—if wood be chosen at all— the finest reds may be aged up to two years before bottling.

Temperature is a vital element in the life cycle of all wines. Interestingly, a wine retains its preference for a particular temperature range all of its life—from fermentation to serving. White wine is fermented at a considerably lower temperature than red (about 55° F.); it is aged in the coolest section of the vintner's cellars and is served chilled. Red wines, fermented at around 80° F., thrive in a warmer, but not too warm atmosphere, and for fullest flavor and bouquet are served at *cool* room temperature. (Room temperature is a deceptive phrase: in terms of wine it originated long ago in Europe, where even today central heating is a rarity. To an American, room temperature is usually 70° to 80° F. For wine it should be between 60° and 70° F.)

Proper aging is the most exacting of the winemakers arts. The timing must be precise, for a wine that is too young will taste rough, harsh. And a wine that has passed its prime will be virtually tasteless, if not worse.

As a general rule, Rosés and delicate whites should be drunk within a year or two of their vintage. The exception to this would be the sturdier white burgundies—the Pinot Chardonnays and Pinot Blancs—which can improve over a three-year span.

The favorite wines of collectors, however, are the reds—the Burgundies and Clarets, the Pinot Noirs, Cabernet Sauvignons, and, sometimes, Zinfandels—which actually "grow" in the cask and later in the bottle, acquiring the subtle complexities of flavor and bouquet that call forth superlatives from the connoisseur.

Wine experts are generally in agreement that Americans drink their finest wines too soon, not allowing them to even approach their peak quality. This appears to be true for a variety of reasons. First, the bottled wine is placed on the market after the minimum amount of bottle aging. From the vintner's point of view, this is sound economics, since most states levy yearly taxes on a winery's inventory—whether or not much of that inventory was in stock the previous year and taxed then. Thus, while European winemakers can reserve their best vintages, letting them age in their own cellars and, incidentally, grow in value with each passing year, American vintners are virtually compelled to distribute their taxable inventories each year. As a result, the wine that arrives at the retailer is drinkable, often even excellent, but in many cases, it is a potentially great wine whose early promise will never be fulfilled. Since there is little likelihood that this situation will change in the near future, it is up to the wine lover to help these fine wines achieve their potential; thus, the importance—and the growing popularity—of the home wine cellar. Americans, who once bought a bottle or two of wine for a specific, special occasion, have discovered the pleasure of collecting particular favorites for "laying away"—as well as the convenience of having on hand a selection of wines for enjoyment whenever the occasion, no matter how small, permits.

Sparkling wines, apéritifs, and dessert wines are fermented and aged differently than table wines. The special techniques used to make these wines are described later. But as a general rule, champagne may be drunk as soon as you buy it, as may all of the flavored appetizer wines. Some sherries and ports, on the other hand, improve immeasurably over the years; a really serious collector might well treasure these wines for a generation or more.

Blending

Blending is an important aspect of the winemaker's art. Most of the wines we drink are blends of different wine types and of wines from different years. The winemaker may decide to add some young wine to give freshness and fruitiness to a mature wine. Or he may blend several types to produce a wine with the most favorable characteristics of each.

American wines with European names — Burgundy, Chablis, Claret — are blended of several different wine varieties to produce a wine similar to its European namesake. (There has been criticism of the use of these European place names for American wines. However, no attempt is made to confuse the consumer, since such wines are clearly labeled "California Burgundy" or "New York State Claret." These names came into use in the nineteenth century, when the American wine industry was taking its first baby steps. The winemakers were primarily descendants of European vintners — from France, Italy, Germany, Switzerland — and they made their wines the way their fathers had, attempting to duplicate the bouquet, body, and flavor of the wines they had known in the Old World. They named their wines with the only names they knew; it was not their intention to deceive.)

These "generic" wines differ in body and flavor from brand to brand. Blending maintains the uniform characteristics associated with a particular brand. Your own taste is your best guide. Taste several wines from several different wineries. When you find one you particularly like, you can be sure it will be as pleasing the next time you drink it.

The desire of American vintners to make even better wines resulted in the blending of the finest grape varieties with only a small selection of other wine grapes. The most desirable grapes were the Pinot Noir, which produces the finest Burgundies in France; the Pinot Chardonnay, principal grape of the famous Chablis; Cabernet Sauvignon, from which the noble Bordeaux are made. In America, a varietal wine must, by law, contain at least 51 percent of the grape variety named. (This law might be compared to France's Appellation Controlee, under which a wine named for a certain district — such as Chablis or Bordeaux — must be made entirely of grapes grown within that district.) Most vintners use a much higher percentage, and in some cases, they use only a single grape type to produce a varietal wine. While this practice sometimes yields an exceptional wine, usually the vintage is improved by blending.

Vintages

According to law, if a wine bottled in the United States carries a vintage date, all of the wine in the bottle must have been produced during that year. Because of this law, many vintners decline to date their wines, preferring to blend wines from different years in order to achieve a particular quality. However, largely because the American wine-drinking public is still vintage conscious, due to their experience with European wines, some vintners are putting out limited bottlings of vintage wines.

Eastern wineries claim that, like their European counterparts, they have good years and poor ones, but California has an almost ideal wine climate year after year. Variations are seldom extreme enough to prevent the grapes from maturing on the vine. Even the devastating early frost in the spring of 1970 — though it destroyed a substantial portion of the young berries — had little affect on the *quality* of the wine that year; during the remaining months, the growing season was fine, and though there was less of it, the wine was excellent.

The chief value of a vintage date is that it indicates the wine's age, thus enabling the consumer to judge how soon to drink the wine or how long he may safely let it continue to age in the bottle.

Bottling

After the wine has been aged and blended (if desired), it is ready for bottling. This is a delicate procedure requiring constant attention to prevent overexposure to air and the bacteria which can cause spoilage.

Wine bottles take many forms — from the balloon-shaped Chianti bottle of Italy to the tall, slender, triangle-shaped bottle traditionally associated with the Rioja wines of Spain. Some American wineries have developed special shapes for certain of their "proprietary" labels — wines which carry a registered trademark associated with the particular winery. But generally, the "fifth" bottles of table wines take the traditional shapes originally developed in Europe.

50

The Burgundy bottle – whether for red or white wine – had rounded shoulders and a long neck.

Clarets – or Bordeaux, Cabernets, and Zinfandels – come in square-shouldered bottles with straight sides.

The Rhine or Riesling bottle is extremely tall and slender.

The glass used for wine bottles is usually tinted dark green, brown, or greenish-brown in order to filter out harmful light rays that can spoil the wine.

Wine Labels

To the uninitiated, a wine label can be as intimidating as St. George's dragon, especially when confronted with phrases like *Grand Cru Classé* and *Mis en Bouteille au Château.* You do not have to be a linguist to decipher American wine labels. But you should understand some wine terminology if you ever want to feel truly comfortable with your own selection.

On any wine label, the first and foremost notations are the type of wine and the name of the maker. The latter invariably appears in the largest print on every label. The former is usually second largest. The wine label will also carry one of the following notices in smaller print:

Estate Bottled. These words are found only on premium wines. They mean that *all* of the wine in the bottle was produced from grapes grown at the winery named and bottled by the vineyard owner. Essentially, the term has the same meaning as "Château" on the fine wines of Europe.

Produced and Bottled by . . . This phrase means that at least 75 percent of the wine was produced at the winery where it was also bottled.

Made and Bottled by . . . This phrase indicates that at least 10 percent of the wine was made and bottled by the winery named.

Bottled by . . . This term means that the winery named merely bottled the wine.

Often a specific winegrowing region, such as Napa Valley, Livermore Valley, Finger Lakes, is named on the bottle. This means the wine was produced in that region and was made primarily from grapes grown in that region. On French wines, this regional designation is known as Appellation d' Origine. "Mountain" or "Lake Country" are terms which indicate that at least 75 percent of the grapes were grown in the mountain regions of California or the Lake Country of New York.

There are other phrases to be found on wine labels: "Special Reserve," "Private Stock," "Special Selection," "Founders Wine." These are used by various wineries to designate a particularly distinguished wine. Such wines are few and hard to come by, and you will certainly recognize them, if not by the label, then by the price.

Corks and Corkscrews

In the United States, as in Europe, fine wines are sealed with the traditional cork. No other closure can quite equal it since it maintains a perfect seal so long as it is kept moist, hence the reason for laying bottles on their sides.

Corkscrews have been designed and redesigned over the centuries for efficient and easy removal of corks from wine bottles. The earliest ones relied on brute

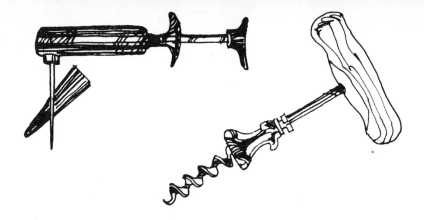

strength. Improvements were made, but for the most part, the removal of corks called for more brawn than brains until the inspired invention of what most of us call "the thing with arms." When the screw of this implement is inserted into the cork, its arms raise up like an angel's wings. One simply pushes them down and the cork comes out, easily and all in one piece.

More favored by maitre d's, sommeliers, and even ordinary waiters is the corkscrew which works with leverage but folds flat for pocket-carrying.

Among other new innovations in cork-removers are the needle-pointed varieties. One kind employs CO_2 cartridges (which somehow just doesn't sound right for injection into wine). Another works with air. The needle of this device is pierced through the cork and air is pumped into the bottle until the cork pops out. It does seem that as in the case of the mousetrap, someone is always trying to build a better corkscrew.

The vast majority of American wines are closed with screw caps. These wines, either in fifth bottles, half-gallon or gallon jugs, will keep for a year or more unopened. There's a definite advantage in storing them: There's no cork to be kept moist, and they can stand upright in your cellar, eliminating the need for a wine rack.

FLAVORED AND
FORTIFIED WINES

"Wine is one of the most civilized things in the world and . . .
it offers a greater range for enjoyment and appreciation than
possibly any other purely sensory thing which may be purchased."
                                                    —Ernest Hemingway

Those wines to which herbs, spices, and other
flavoring ingredients have been added are known as
flavored wines. In this category are the Vermouths,
both sweet and dry, as well as a host of apéritif and
dessert wines, many of them bearing fanciful names
registered by their individual makers.

Those wines to which brandy has been added are
called fortified wines. Among these are the Sherries,
Ports, Madeiras, Muscatels—some of them apéritifs,
most of them after-dinner wines. In the making of
these wines, wine brandy is added to halt the
fermentation while some sugar remains. It also
serves to raise the alcoholic content.

Sherry

Sherry found its first great success in England, the
country that has foretold the success of so many
now-standard drinks.

Originally a product of Spain, it is named for the
Spanish town *Jerez,* the word "Sherry" being an
Anglicization of this name. Sherry is now produced
in most of the winelands of America, but principally
in California and New York. The best Sherries are
made from the Palomino grape.

In the crush and fermentation, the process of making Sherry is no different from that of making any other wine, except that when the desired degree of dryness is achieved, fermentation is stopped by the addition of some grape brandy. For Cream Sherries, fermentation is halted while the wine still contains about 10 to 12 percent sugar. Very dry Sherries are allowed to continue to ferment until only 2 percent sugar, or even less, remains.

It is the practice of many American manufacturers to store the new wine which has been drawn off the pulps in wooden vats or casks and heat it to about 120° F. The wine is kept at this temperature for as long as a year, then cooled and set aside to age. This heating process produces an acceptable Sherry. However, some American winemakers have substituted the classic *flor* process, traditionally used to make the world's great Sherries.

In the *flor* process, the *flor* yeast is laid atop the new wine after fermentation has been halted by the addition of grape brandy. The *flor* grows, covering the wine with a crust. Those wines on which the *flor* flourishes become Finos, the dry Sherries; those with small amounts of *flor* become the sweet Sherries, or Olorosos. After the *flor* is removed and discarded, the alcoholic content of the wine is again adjusted by the addition of grape brandy. It varies from about 15 percent in the Finos to 18 percent or more in the Olorosos. Finally, the wines are transferred to wooden casks for aging and blending by means of the Solera system, which is unique to the making of Sherry.

At its simplest, a Solera is a stack of casks placed one above the other, pyramid-like, in rows four or five casks high. The oldest wine is in the bottom casks, the newest in the top ones. As the matured wine is drawn from the bottom barrel, wine from the second barrel is added to it, wine from the third barrel is added to the second, and so on. To replace the wine drawn from the top barrel, still newer Sherry is added. In this way, there is a constant blending of old and new that can continue for years, producing the special flavor and uniform characteristics we expect of Sherry, bottle after bottle. There are no vintage years in Sherry.

Cooking with Sherry

Sherry is the most versatile of all wine in cooking. (Do not be misled into buying "cooking" Sherry at the local grocery. Invariably, this is an inferior wine to which salt has been added to render it undrinkable and thus take it out of the alcoholic beverage class. Ironically, it is usually more expensive than a good drinking Sherry.)

Sherry — dry, medium, or cream — can be added to virtually every dish to make it better. To soups it imparts a distinctive nutty flavor. It lends an irresistible aroma and flavor to the best beef stew, and chicken steeped in Sherry is not only elegant, but simple and easy to make. Nearly every sauce, every gravy, given a dash of Sherry, will acquire a deliciously subtle nuance.

SHERRY

SHERRIED LAMB STEW

2 tablespoons bacon drippings or other fat
2 pounds boneless lamb shoulder, cubed
½ cup ground or minced onion
3 tablespoons flour
1 cup beef stock (canned or bouillon-cube broth
  may be used)
½ cup Sherry
1 teaspoon Worcestershire sauce
¼ teaspoon paprika
Salt and pepper
4 carrots, diced
1 cup dairy sour cream
1 (1-lb.) can tiny whole white onions, drained
1 (12-oz.) package frozen peas, cooked and
  drained
2 tablespoons chopped parsley

Heat bacon drippings in a Dutch oven or other heavy
kettle. Add lamb and onion; sauté, stirring
frequently, until lamb is nicely browned. Sprinkle
flour over meat and blend well. Add stock and wine
and cook, stirring constantly, until sauce boils and
thickens. Season with Worcestershire sauce, paprika,
salt, and pepper. Add carrots. Cover and simmer
gently, stirring occasionally, for 1½ hours, or until
lamb is very tender. Add sour cream. (If sauce is now
a little thinner than you like it, blend 1 tablespoon
flour with an equal amount of soft butter or
margarine, add to contents of Dutch oven, and
simmer until sauce thickens.) Add onions, peas, and
parsley. Taste and add additional salt if needed.
Heat thoroughly before serving. *Serves 4.*

SHERRIED AVOCADO-CRABMEAT COCKTAIL

$\frac{1}{2}$ cup catsup
$\frac{1}{4}$ cup mayonnaise
$\frac{1}{4}$ cup Sherry*
1 teaspoon lemon juice
Dash of cayenne
1 cup flaked fresh or 1 ($6\frac{1}{2}$-oz.) can crabmeat
1 cup diced avocado
$\frac{1}{2}$ cup finely diced celery

Mix catsup, mayonnaise, wine, lemon juice, and cayenne. Beat with a rotary or electric beater until well blended. Chill for an hour or more. Shortly before serving time, mix sauce with the crabmeat, avocado, and celery. Spoon into 6 cocktail glasses. Serve at once. (Note: Lobster, shrimp, or tuna may be substituted for the crabmeat with equally good results.) *Serves 6.*

*Unless otherwise specified, use medium or cocktail Sherry.

ESCALLOPED CHICKEN AND AVOCADO

1 small white onion, finely chopped
3 tablespoons butter
3 tablespoons flour
½ teaspoon salt
1 cup cream
¾ cup milk
¼ cup dry Sherry
2 cups diced cooked chicken (or turkey or ham)
1 (3-oz.) can whole or sliced mushrooms
1 cup grated aged Cheddar cheese
⅛ teaspoon dried dill or rosemary
1 large avocado

Cook onion slowly in butter until soft but not
browned. Blend in flour and salt. Slowly stir in
cream and milk; continue cooking and stirring until
mixture boils and thickens. Blend in wine, chicken,
mushrooms, about half the cheese, and dill or
rosemary. Turn mixture into a shallow baking dish
or individual bakers. Cut avocado in half; remove
seed and skin. Cut fruit into slices and arrange
over creamed chicken; top with remaining cheese.
Bake in a slow oven (300° F.) until cheese melts,
about 5 to 10 minutes. *Serves 4.*

SHERRIED LEMON SOUP

3 pounds chicken pieces
2 quarts water
2 bay leaves
1 tablespoon salt
$\frac{1}{4}$ teaspoon pepper
2 onions, quartered
1 clove garlic
1 cup Cream Sherry
2 tablespoons lemon juice
6 or 8 thin lemon slices
$\frac{1}{4}$ teaspoon crushed tarragon leaves

Place chicken pieces, water, bay leaves, salt, pepper, onion, and garlic in large kettle. Bring to a boil, lower heat, and simmer (covered) until chicken is tender, about $1\frac{1}{2}$ to 2 hours. Remove chicken pieces from broth. When cool enough to handle, cut meat from bones. Strain broth. Combine strained broth with Sherry, lemon juice and slices, and tarragon. Add chicken meat and simmer about 10 minutes. Serve with a lemon slice in each cup or bowl.
Serves 6.

SCALLOPED OYSTERS PACIFICA

1 pint small oysters
3 tablespoons butter
3 tablespoons sifted flour
1 cup cream
$\frac{1}{3}$ cup dry Sherry
1 teaspoon lemon juice
$\frac{1}{4}$ teaspoon grated lemon rind
Dash of nutmeg
Seasoned salt and pepper
2 cups croutons ($\frac{1}{2}$-inch bread cubes toasted dry
　and golden brown)
$\frac{1}{3}$ cup grated or shredded Parmesan cheese
Paprika

Drain oysters, saving liquid. Melt butter, stir in
flour. Add cream and cook, stirring, until mixture
boils and thickens. Stir in wine, lemon juice and
rind, nutmeg, oyster liquid, and salt and pepper.
Arrange half the oysters in a greased casserole;
top with half the croutons and half the sauce. Repeat
layers. Sprinkle Parmesan cheese over the top and
dust with paprika. Bake in a hot oven (450° F.) about
25 minutes. *Serves 4.*

SHERRIED STUFFED LOBSTER

1 envelope unflavored gelatin
¼ cup cold water
½ cup hot canned consommé
¾ cup cold canned consommé
⅓ cup Sherry
1 teaspoon lemon juice
¼ teaspoon Worcestershire sauce
Salt and pepper to taste
1½ cups cooked lobster
½ cup finely cut celery

Soften gelatin in the cold water for 5 minutes. Dissolve in the hot consommé. Add cold consommé, wine, lemon juice, Worcestershire sauce, salt, and pepper. Chill until mixture begins to thicken, then fold in lobster and celery. Turn into 6 individual molds that have been rinsed with cold water. Chill until firm. Unmold on crisp salad greens and serve with Russian Dressing (below).

Russian Dressing: Mix ¾ cup mayonnaise, ¼ cup chili sauce, 1 teaspoon lemon juice, ¼ teaspoon paprika, and salt to taste. Add 1 tablespoon each: chopped capers, green pepper, and pimiento. Cover and chill for an hour or more before serving.
Serves 6.

LIVER DELECTA

1 pound sliced beef liver
4 tablespoons butter or margarine
3 tablespoons flour
1 cup canned consommé or bouillon-cube broth
$\frac{1}{2}$ cup cream or evaporated milk
$\frac{1}{4}$ cup Sherry
$\frac{1}{2}$ teaspoon Worcestershire sauce
Salt and pepper
2 tablespoons chopped parsley

Remove skin from liver slices; cut slices in strips or squares. Heat 3 tablespoons of the butter in a large skillet; add liver and sauté *quickly* for 2 or 3 minutes (no longer!), stirring frequently. Remove liver from skillet. Add the remaining 1 tablespoon butter to drippings in skillet; blend in flour; add consommé and cream; cook, stirring constantly, until mixture is thickened and smooth. Add Sherry, Worcestershire sauce, salt, pepper, and parsley. Add liver to sauce and heat just until piping hot. Serve at once on toast or with rice. *Serves 4.*

HAM AND HOMINY

$\frac{1}{2}$ cup chopped green pepper
1 (4-oz.) can mushroom stems and pieces,
   drained
4 tablespoons butter or margarine
5 tablespoons flour
2 cups milk
$\frac{1}{3}$ cup Sherry
$\frac{1}{2}$ teaspoon Worcestershire sauce
Salt and pepper
1 (No. $2\frac{1}{2}$) can hominy, drained
1 (12-oz.) can chopped ham, diced
$\frac{1}{2}$ cup grated Cheddar cheese
Paprika

Sauté green pepper and mushrooms slowly in butter
for 5 minutes. Blend in flour; add milk and cook,
stirring constantly, until mixture boils and thickens.
Remove from heat; add Sherry, Worcestershire sauce,
salt, and pepper. Mix sauce with the hominy and
ham. Turn into a greased casserole; sprinkle with
grated cheese and paprika. Bake in a moderately hot
oven (375° F.) for about 25 minutes, or until bubbly
and delicately browned. *Serves 4.*

OLD-STYLE YAM-APPLE-SAUSAGE CASSEROLE

1/4 cup Sherry
1/4 cup brown sugar (packed)
2 tablespoons melted butter or margarine
1 teaspoon salt
4 large yams, boiled, peeled, and sliced
2 cups sliced apples
1 pound link sausage

Mix wine, sugar, butter, and salt. Arrange alternate layers of yams and apples in a greased baking dish; sprinkle each layer with some of the wine mixture; cover and bake in a moderately hot oven (450°F.) for 30 minutes. Meanwhile, simmer sausages in water to cover for 10 minutes; drain thoroughly. At the end of the 30-minute baking period, place sausages on top of yams and apples; continue baking, uncovered, for about 40 minutes, or until apples are tender and sausages are nicely browned. *Serves 4.*

70

CARROTS A L'INDIENNE

3 cups sliced carrots
Boiling salted water
½ cup Sherry
¼ teaspoon grated orange rind
⅓ cup orange juice
1 tablespoon cornstarch
½ teaspoon seasoned salt
2 teaspoons sugar
¼ teaspoon powdered ginger
⅛ teaspoon curry powder
2 tablespoons butter or margarine
1 tablespoon lemon juice

Cook carrots in boiling salted water just until tender,
about 10 to 15 minutes. Meanwhile, combine Sherry,
orange rind and juice, cornstarch, salt, sugar, ginger,
and curry powder in a small saucepan. Cook, stirring,
until mixture boils and thickens. Stir in butter and
lemon juice; heat a few minutes longer. Drain
carrots well and combine with sauce. *Serves 6.*

SHERRIED SPINACH SOUFFLÉ

1 (12-oz.) package frozen chopped spinach or
  1 cup chopped cooked fresh spinach
¾ cup milk
¼ cup biscuit mix
¼ cup Sherry
⅛ teaspoon nutmeg
3 eggs, separated
1 teaspoon salt
¼ teaspoon cream of tartar

Cook spinach according to package directions. Drain
thoroughly, pressing out all excess water. Stir a
little of the milk into biscuit mix to make a smooth
paste. Gradually blend in remaining milk. Cook,
stirring, over direct heat until mixture boils
thoroughly and is thick. Stir in Sherry and nutmeg.
Remove from heat. Beat egg yolks lightly. Stir hot
cooked mixture into yolks; blend in spinach.
Combine egg whites, salt, and cream of tartar and
beat until stiff. Fold into first mixture. Turn into
ungreased 1-quart soufflé dish or straight-sided
casserole. Set in pan of hot water. Bake in moderate
oven (350° F.) about 50 minutes, or until knife
inserted in center comes out clean. Serve at once.
Serves 6.

HOLIDAY MUFFINS

2 cups sifted all-purpose flour
$\frac{1}{3}$ cup sugar
3 teaspoons baking powder
1 teaspoon salt
$\frac{1}{4}$ teaspoon mace
$\frac{1}{2}$ cup chopped walnuts
1 egg
1 tablespoon grated orange rind
$\frac{2}{3}$ cup milk
$\frac{1}{3}$ cup Sherry
$\frac{1}{4}$ cup melted shortening

Sift flour with sugar, baking powder, salt, and mace.
Add walnuts. Beat egg lightly, add orange rind,
milk, Sherry, and shortening. Stir into dry mixture,
blending only until all of flour is moistened. Spoon
into greased muffin pans. Bake in hot oven (425° F.)
about 20 minutes. Serve hot. *Makes 1 dozen.*

PECAN FRUIT CAKE

$\frac{1}{2}$ cup golden raisins
2 cups (1 lb.) mixed candied fruit
1 cup Sherry
2$\frac{1}{2}$ cups sifted flour
1 teaspoon freshly grated nutmeg
$\frac{1}{2}$ teaspoon baking powder
$\frac{7}{8}$ cup butter or margarine
$\frac{1}{2}$ cup brown sugar (packed)
1 cup sugar
3 eggs
1 pound (4$\frac{1}{2}$ cups) pecan halves

Soak fruit overnight in Sherry. Sift flour with
nutmeg and baking powder. Cream butter and
sugars until light and fluffy. Add eggs one at a time
and beat well. Fold in flour mixture alternately with
soaked fruits. Add pecans. Mix well and turn into
paper-lined, greased tube pan. Bake in slow oven
(275° F.) about 3 hours, or until cake tests done. Cool
and store.

BROWN VELVET BANANA PIE

1 (9-inch) pastry shell
1 (6-oz.) package semisweet chocolate bits
3 tablespoons sugar
$\frac{1}{4}$ teaspoon cinnamon
2 teaspoons instant coffee powder
$\frac{1}{8}$ teaspoon salt
$\frac{1}{4}$ cup Sherry
4 eggs, separated
3 bananas

Bake, cool, and chill the pastry shell. Combine chocolate bits with sugar, cinnamon, coffee powder, salt, and Sherry in top of double boiler. Place over hot water. Cook and stir until chocolate is melted and mixture blended. Remove from heat and cool. Beat in egg yolks, one at a time, until thoroughly blended. Beat egg whites until stiff but not dry. Gently fold into chocolate mixture. Peel and slice 2 bananas. Sprinkle lightly with additional Sherry. Arrange sliced bananas in bottom of chilled pastry shell. Spread chocolate mixture on top; refrigerate several hours until firm. When ready to serve, peel and slice the remaining banana; arrange over top of pie.

MEAT BALLS IN CELERY SAUCE

⅓ pound each: ground beef, veal and lean pork
1 cup crushed cornflakes
1¾ cups milk
1 egg, slightly beaten
1 tablespoon minced onion
¼ teaspoon nutmeg
Salt and pepper
2 tablespoons bacon drippings or other fat
1 can condensed cream of celery soup
⅓ cup Sherry
2 tablespoons chopped parsley

Mix meat, cornflakes, ¾ cup milk, egg, onion, nutmeg, 1 teaspoon salt, and ¼ teaspoon pepper. Shape into walnut-sized balls. Heat bacon drippings in a large, heavy skillet; brown balls nicely on all sides. Remove balls and pour off all drippings from skillet. Combine soup, remaining 1 cup milk, Sherry and parsley in skillet; season to taste with salt and pepper; heat to simmering. Add balls; cover and simmer gently, stirring occasionally, for 30 minutes. Good with noodles or rice. *Serves 5 or 6.*

SHERRIED BAKED BANANAS

4 green-tipped bananas
$1/4$ cup Sherry
2 tablespoons lemon juice
$1/4$ teaspoon nutmeg
Dash of salt
$1/4$ cup brown sugar (packed)

Peel bananas; cut into halves lengthwise and into halves or thirds crosswise. Arrange in shallow baking dish. Combine Sherry, lemon juice, nutmeg, and salt and drizzle over fruit. Sprinkle sugar over all. Bake in moderate oven (350° F.) for 18 to 20 minutes, just until bananas are tender. Baste occasionally as bananas are cooling. *Serves 4.*

SAVORY BRAISED BEEF

2 pounds round steak, cut 1-inch thick
$\frac{1}{3}$ cup flour
Salt and pepper to taste
3 tablespoons bacon drippings or other fat
1 can condensed tomato soup
$\frac{1}{2}$ cup Sherry
1 small onion, minced
$\frac{1}{2}$ cup sour cream
2 tablespoons chopped parsley

Remove skin and fat from meat. Mix flour, salt, and
pepper; rub mixture into meat, then pound meat
with the edge of a heavy plate or with a wooden
mallet. Cut meat in strips about 2 inches long and
the width of a pencil. Heat bacon drippings in a
large, heavy skillet; add meat and brown nicely on
all sides. Add soup, Sherry and onion; cover tightly
and simmer gently for about $1\frac{1}{4}$ hours, or until meat
is very tender, stirring frequently. Add sour cream
and parsley; taste and add salt and pepper if
necessary. Heat thoroughly and serve at once. Serve
with rice, noodles, or mashed or baked potatoes.
Serves 5 or 6.

INDIVIDUAL BARBECUED MEAT LOAVES WITH SHERRY SAUCE

1½ pounds ground beef
1 cup soft bread crumbs
1 egg, slightly beaten
2 tablespoons grated onion
1½ teaspoons salt
¼ teaspoon pepper
½ (8 oz.) can tomato sauce

Mix all ingredients together lightly but thoroughly. Shape into 4 little meat loaves; place in a greased shallow baking pan. Bake in a moderate oven (350° F.) for 1 hour. Drain most of fat from the pan. Pour Sherry Barbecue Sauce (below) over loaves. Continue baking at 350° F. for ½ hour, basting loaves frequently with the sauce.

Sherry Barbecue Sauce:

1 tablespoon cornstarch
2 tablespoons brown sugar
½ (8 oz.) can tomato sauce
¾ cup Sherry
¾ cup beef stock (canned or bouillon-cube broth may be used)
1 tablespoon wine vinegar
1 teaspoon prepared mustard
Salt to taste

Mix cornstarch and sugar in a saucepan; add remaining ingredients, mixing until smooth. Stir over medium heat until sauce boils and thickens. Pour over meat loaves as directed above. *Serves 4.*

STEAKIES

These patties really are delicious, and there's lots of good gravy to spoon over the toast or potatoes. A relatively inexpensive dish. Only a very hearty eater could get away with more than one of these, we think.

1 pound ground beef
1 cup (firmly packed) grated soft bread crumbs
2 eggs, slightly beaten
$\frac{1}{2}$ cup cream
$\frac{1}{4}$ cup Sherry
$\frac{1}{2}$ cup finely chopped onion
$\frac{1}{4}$ cup chopped parsley
1 teaspoon salt
$\frac{1}{4}$ teaspoon pepper
3 tablespoons bacon drippings or other fat
2 ($10\frac{3}{4}$-oz.) cans beef gravy
2 tablespoons California Sherry
1 (4-oz.) can mushroom stems and pieces,
    drained (optional)

In a mixing bowl combine beef, bread crumbs, eggs, cream, the $\frac{1}{4}$ cup wine, onion, parsley, salt and pepper; mix lightly but thoroughly. Cover and chill mixture several hours or overnight to make it easier to handle. Shape chilled mixture into 6 fat patties, allowing about $\frac{1}{2}$ cup mixture per patty. Heat bacon drippings in a large, heavy skillet; brown patties slowly on both sides. Pour off fat from skillet. Add gravy, the 2 tablespoons wine and mushrooms (if used); cover and simmer very gently for 45 minutes, turning and basting patties several times. Serve on toast, or with mashed or baked potatoes. *Serves 6.*

SHERRIED CHICKEN LIVERS

1 pound chicken livers
4 tablespoons butter or margarine
2 tablespoons chopped onion
2 tablespoons flour
1 (10¾-oz.) can beef gravy
¼ cup Sherry
1 tablespoon canned tomato paste
Salt and pepper
1 (4-oz.) can mushroom stems and pieces,
   drained
2 tablespoons chopped parsley

Cut chicken livers in halves. Melt butter in a large,
heavy skillet; sauté onion until tender and golden.
Add chicken livers; sauté gently about 5 minutes, or
until lightly browned, turning frequently. Remove
livers from pan. Add flour to drippings and blend
well; add gravy and wine; cook, stirring, until
mixture boils and thickens. Blend in tomato paste;
season with salt and pepper. Just before serving, add
livers, mushrooms and parsley to sauce; heat
gently but thoroughly. Serve on toast, or with rice
or noodles. *Serves 4.*

GINGERED BARBECUED SPARERIBS

1 (8-oz.) can tomato sauce
¼ cup Sherry
¼ cup brown sugar
1 tablespoon Worcestershire sauce
2 tablespoons wine vinegar
1 medium-sized onion, chopped
1 clove garlic, minced or crushed
1 teaspoon salt
½ teaspoon chili powder
½ teaspoon celery salt
½ teaspoon dry mustard
⅛ teaspoon pepper
6 pounds country-style ribs (2 sides)
2 tablespoons chopped candied ginger

Combine all ingredients except ribs and ginger.
Cover and simmer about 15 minutes. Use for basting
sauce for spareribs. Grill ribs over very low coals
about 1½ hours, basting and turning frequently.
When ready to serve, sprinkle ribs with about 2
tablespoons finely chopped candied ginger. *Makes
6 to 8 servings.*

BAKED NOODLES PAPRIKA

½ pound wide egg noodles
2 tablespoons butter or margarine
2 tablespoons flour
1 cup dairy sour cream
⅓ cup dry Sherry
1 cup cottage cheese
1 teaspoon Worcestershire sauce
1 teaspoon paprika
Dash of garlic powder
Salt and pepper
2 tablespoons grated Parmesan cheese

Cook noodles in boiling salted water until tender;
drain. Melt butter and stir in flour; add sour cream
and Sherry; cook, stirring constantly, until mixture
boils and thickens. Add cottage cheese, Worcestershire sauce, paprika, garlic powder, salt and pepper.
Combine this mixture with the noodles. Turn into
a greased baking dish; sprinkle with Parmesan
cheese. Bake, uncovered, in a moderate oven (350° F.)
for 40 minutes. *Serves 6.*

DILLY SALMON PIE

Pastry for 2-crust (8 or 9-inch) pie
1 tablespoon butter
1 tablespoon flour
¼ teaspoon salt
¾ cup rich milk
¼ cup dry Sherry
1 (16-oz.) can red salmon
3 hard-cooked eggs
½ teaspoon dried dill
Salt and pepper
3 green onions, finely chopped

Divide pastry in half. Roll half to 9-inch diameter
and fit into an 8-inch pie pan. Roll remaining pastry
to an 8-inch circle. (If 9-inch pan is used, roll pastry
to 10 inches for bottom, 9 inches for top.) Melt butter
and blend in flour and salt. Gradually stir in milk;
cook and stir until sauce is thickened. Blend in
Sherry and set aside. Drain and flake salmon,
removing bones and skin. Turn into pastry shell.
Slice eggs and arrange over salmon. Sprinkle with
dill, salt and pepper and green onions. Pour cooled
sauch over salmon. Place pastry round over filling.
Turn rim of bottom crust inward towards center.
Flute edge and prick top. Bake in hot oven (425° F.)
30 to 35 minutes, or until well browned. *Serves 5.*

SHERRY CREAM PARFAIT

1 envelope unflavored gelatin
$\frac{1}{4}$ cup cold water
$\frac{1}{2}$ cup sugar
$\frac{3}{4}$ cup Sherry
2 egg whites, stiffly beaten
$\frac{1}{2}$ cup heavy cream, whipped
12 ladyfingers
$\frac{1}{3}$ cup crushed peanut brittle

Soften gelatin in the cold water for 5 minutes;
dissolve over hot water; add sugar and stir until
dissolved. Remove from heat; add Sherry; chill.
When mixture begins to thicken, fold in beaten egg
whites and whipped cream, blending gently but
thoroughly. Split ladyfingers; line each of 6 sherbet
glasses with 4 halves, rounded side out. Spoon in
Sherry-cream mixture; sprinkle crushed peanut
brittle over the top. Chill until firm. Serve plain or
topped with whipped cream. *Serves 6.*

SALMON FLORENTINE

4 tablespoons butter or margarine
5 tablespoons flour
1 cup light cream
$^3/_4$ cup chicken stock (canned or bouillon-cube
  broth may be used)
$^1/_4$ cup Sherry
2 tablespoons mayonnaise
$^1/_2$ cup grated Parmesan cheese
$^1/_2$ teaspoon grated lemon rind
$^1/_2$ teaspoon Worcestershire sauce
Salt, pepper and paprika to taste
2 cups (firmly packed) *thoroughly* drained,
  chopped, cooked or canned spinach
1 (1 lb.) can salmon

Melt butter and stir in flour; add cream and stock;
cook, stirring constantly, until mixture boils and
thickens. Add wine, mayonnaise, $^1/_4$ cup of the cheese,
lemon rind, Worcestershire sauce, salt, pepper and
paprika. Mix $^1/_2$ cup or so of this sauce with the
spinach; spread in bottom of a greased 10 by 6 by
2-inch baking dish. Drain salmon. Remove bones
and skin. Separate into bite-size pieces. Add salmon
to remaining sauce. Pour over spinach. Sprinkle
remaining $^1/_4$ cup cheese over the top. Dust with
paprika. Bake in a moderately hot oven (375° F.) for
about 25 minutes or until bubbly and delicately
brown. *Serves 4 or 5.*

BOUNTIFUL MEAT PATTIES

1 pound ground beef
$\frac{1}{2}$ pound fresh pork
1 cup (firmly packed) grated soft bread crumbs
$\frac{1}{2}$ cup uncooked rice
1 small onion, chopped
1 cup milk
1 egg, well beaten
$1\frac{1}{2}$ teaspoon salt
$\frac{1}{2}$ teaspoon pepper
$\frac{1}{4}$ teaspoon mace
$\frac{1}{8}$ teaspoon allspice
1 can ($1\frac{1}{4}$ cups) condensed cream of mushroom
    soup
$\frac{1}{2}$ cup milk
$\frac{1}{3}$ cup Sherry

Combine beef, pork, bread crumbs, rice, onion, milk,
egg, salt, pepper and spices, mixing lightly but
thoroughly. Shape into 6 fat patties and place in a
single layer in a baking dish. Combine soup, milk
and wine; heat to simmering; pour over patties.
Cover and bake in a moderate oven (350° F.) for
1 hour, turning and basting patties several times
after the first half hour of cooking. *Serves 6.*

Port

Port, the ultimate after-dinner wine, has a whole ritual surrounding it. In almost every Victorian novel there is at least one scene where the ladies retire to the drawing room, leaving the men to their cigars, their politics, and their port. There is even a special way of serving port: The host serves the guest to his right, then himself, then passes the bottle to his left, around the table, clockwise. And so it goes, 'round and 'round, at least twice, more often three times.

Port was born in Portugal and, like sherry, was popularized by the English. During the wars with Spain, the proper Britishers felt it unpatriotic to drink the classic wine of Jerez and turned to neighboring Portugal to satisfy their thirst.

As in Europe, the best American Ports are produced from the Tinta Madeira grape, but other Tinta varieties may be used instead. Like all fortified wines, Port begins with a base wine in which fermentation has been halted while some sweetness remains.*

Ports are variously labeled Ruby, Tawny, and, rarely, Vintage. Vintage is the finest of Ports, made entirely of grapes harvested in an especially good year, aged only a few years in wood, and then bottled and laid away for as long as forty to fifty years, by which time it will have achieved a matchless flavor and smoothness.

*Port is actually a refortified wine. Brandy is used at the initial stage to stop fermentation, and just before bottling, more brandy is added to further raise the alcoholic content of the wine.

Vintage Port must be handled with reverence. The reclining bottle must never be jostled because the wine throws a "crust" of sediment which settles along the "down" side of the bottle. If the crust is disturbed, it mixes with the wine. When serving Vintage Port, one decants it very carefully, being careful to stop pouring when the sediment begins to creep toward the neck of the bottle.

It's nice to know these things, but it is unlikely you'll ever be called upon to use your knowledge, since Vintage Port is so great a rarity and so prized by collectors (who seem to have a direct line of communication to the grapevines of the world) that it seldom reaches the ordinary table.

There is no need to feel overly deprived though. Tawny Port, in much more plentiful supply, is rich, mellow, and full-bodied. Even connoisseurs content themselves with it on most occasions. (One wonders, in fact, how much real enjoyment the rarest wines offer their owners. There is, of course, that moment of pride when the prized bottle is presented to one's guests, but it must be just that—a moment. Then everyone works very hard to discover every nuance the liquid treasure has to offer. And then—it's gone!) With Tawny Port, one can relax and enjoy, with little worry about some exquisitely unexpected flavor slipping by. There's plenty more of the wine, and many more opportunities to discover each elusive quality.

Tawny Port, which takes its name from its russet, or reddish gold, color, may be made entirely of grapes harvested in one year. But most often, it is a blend of wines from several different years, as are most Ports and all Sherries. Vintage Port is bottled young; Tawny is aged eight to twelve years in wooden casks. Since wine ages faster in wood than in the bottle, Tawny Port is ready to drink when you buy it, although the patient collector who "lays away" a few bottles for a few more years, will reap his rewards in a finer, smoother wine. Tawny Port does not throw a crust, thus it can withstand considerably more casual treatment than the delicate Vintage.

Ruby Port is also named for its color, a deep ruby red. American Ports simply labeled "Port" are usually Ruby. This is the youngest and least expensive of all Ports, and bears the least resemblance to its European parent. It's a pleasant, if undistinguished, wine.

White Port is almost as rare as Vintage, and most Port enthusiasts claim it is not Port at all. Very pale in color, drier than other Ports, it is frequently used as an aperitif. Only a very small quantity is bottled by American winemakers, and it is generally regarded more as a novelty than a wine for serious consideration.

Cooking with Port

Port is almost as ubiquitous as Sherry in cooking. It imparts an incomparably rich, fruity flavor to appropriate dishes—those which can stand up to its full-bodied consistency—and there are many.

PORT

CITRUS CHICKEN WITH PORT

1 (2½-lb.) frying chicken
2 tablespoons oil or butter
Salt
Pepper
½ cup orange juice
½ cup Port
1 tablespoon fresh lemon juice
2 teaspoons cornstarch
1 tablespoon cold water

Have chicken cut into serving pieces. Brown slowly
on all sides in heated oil. Sprinkle with salt and
pepper. Combine orange juice, wine, and lemon juice,
pour over chicken, cover and bake in moderately hot
oven (375° F.) about 30 minutes. Remove chicken
pieces. Blend cornstarch with water and stir into
drippings. Cook and stir over moderate heat until
sauce boils thoroughly and is thickened. Serve sauce
over chicken. *Serves 4.*

CHEESE TOWER

$\frac{1}{2}$ pound American cheese, grated
$\frac{1}{4}$ pound blue cheese, crumbled
1 (3-oz.) package cream cheese
$\frac{1}{2}$ cup Port
$\frac{1}{2}$ teaspoon Worcestershire sauce
$\frac{1}{2}$ teaspoon paprika
Salt and onion salt to taste
Dash of garlic powder
Dash of cayenne

Have cheeses at room temperature. In a bowl blend all cheeses well with a fork. Gradually beat in wine; add seasonings. Beat (preferably with an electric beater or blender) until mixture is smooth and creamy. Pack into lightly oiled fancy mold, if desired. Store, covered, in the refrigerator. *Makes 2½ cups.*

CHICKEN LIVERS IN PORT

2 small green onions, finely chopped
$\frac{1}{4}$ cup butter or margarine
$\frac{1}{2}$ pound chicken livers
$\frac{1}{4}$ teaspoon fresh sage, or $\frac{1}{8}$ teaspoon ground
    sage
$\frac{1}{4}$ teaspoon salt
1 tablespoon lemon juice
$\frac{1}{3}$ cup Port
$\frac{1}{8}$ teaspoon freshly ground pepper

Sauté onions in melted butter a few minutes. Add livers; sauté 3 to 5 minutes, depending on size of livers. Bruise sage; add along with salt, lemon juice, Port, and pepper. Cook slowly about 8 minutes, stirring occasionally. Correct seasoning and serve on toast. The menu might include a tossed green salad with oil and wine vinegar dressing; toasted French bread; and dessert of Port, apple wedges, and a few walnuts. *Serves 2.*

JELLIED CRANBERRY-TURKEY SALAD

1 cup bottled cranberry juice
1 (3-oz.) package raspberry or cherry gelatin
½ cup Port
Tiny sprigs romaine or other lettuce
Turkey Salad

Heat cranberry juice to boiling. Stir in gelatin until
dissolved. Remove from heat; add Port and cool.
Turn into large wine glasses, goblets, or individual
molds. Chill until firm. When ready to serve,
arrange small spears of romaine in each glass. Spoon
in turkey salad. If small molds are used, turn out on
crisp greens and surround with salad mixture.

Turkey Salad: Combine 1½ cups bite-size pieces
cooked turkey (or chicken), ¾ cup chopped celery,
2 tablespoons chopped green onion, ¾ teaspoon
seasoned salt, and ⅛ teaspoon seasoned or plain
pepper. Chill several hours. Add 3 or 4 tablespoons
mayonnaise and ½ cup seedless grapes just before
serving. *Serves 4.*

STEAK SUPREME

4 beef fillets, about 2 inches thick
6 tablespoons butter
Salt and pepper
$\frac{1}{2}$ cup Port
$\frac{1}{4}$ cup undiluted consommé
3 tablespoons chopped green onions

Sauté fillets quickly in butter over medium-high
heat to brown. Lower heat, and cook until medium
rare. Season with salt and pepper. Arrange fillets on
hot platter. Add wine and consommé to pan in
which meat was cooked. Heat and pour over steaks.
Sprinkle with chopped onion. *Serves 4.*

PORTED MUSHROOM BEEF

1 pound beef top round steak
2 tablespoons butter or margarine
1 cup sliced fresh mushrooms
1 teaspoon salt
$\frac{1}{8}$ teaspoon pepper
$\frac{1}{2}$ teaspoon grated lemon rind
$\frac{1}{4}$ teaspoon crushed marjoram leaves
$\frac{3}{4}$ cup Port
$\frac{1}{4}$ cup water
2 teaspoons cornstarch

Cut beef into 1-inch cubes. Sauté lightly in butter until browned. Push to one side of pan; add mushrooms and brown lightly. Add all remaining ingredients except cornstarch. Stir to blend. Cover and simmer over low heat until beef is tender, about 50 to 60 minutes. Remove cover, blend in cornstarch mixed with an additional tablespoon of Port. Cook, stirring, until sauce boils and thickens. Serve over noodles or rice. *Serves 4.*

PORTED BERRY JAM

1 (10-oz.) package frozen strawberries
2 (10-oz.) packages frozen raspberries
3 cups sugar
⅓ cup lemon juice
¼ cup Port

Partially thaw frozen berries. Combine with sugar,
cover and let stand 1 hour, stirring now and then.
Boil mixture rapidly for 8 minutes. Remove from
heat. Add lemon juice and Port; boil 2 minutes
longer. (This is a soft jam with fresh fruit flavor.)
Makes 4 cups.

RUBY SALAD MOLD

1 (6-oz.) package raspberry gelatin
1½ cups boiling water
1 cup cranberry juice cocktail
½ cup Port
1 (8¾-oz.) can pineapple tidbits
½ cup finely chopped celery
2 tablespoons finely chopped green or mild
** onion**
1 cup peeled, diced apple
Crisp salad greens
Preserved kumquats (optional)

Dissolve gelatin in boiling water, stirring until
completely dissolved. Add cranberry juice cocktail,
Port, and undrained pineapple tidbits. Chill until
mixture begins to thicken. Fold in celery, onion,
and apple. Turn into a lightly oiled 1-quart mold.
Chill until firm. Unmold on crisp salad greens and
garnish with preserved kumquats, if desired. Serve
plain or with mayonnaise. (Note: When using
unusually tall molds, decrease water to 1 cup.)
Serves 8.

BEET-APPLE SALAD

1 (No. 303) can shoestring beets
1 (3-oz.) package lemon gelatin
1 cup hot water
⅓ cup Port
1 tablespoon lemon juice
1 teaspoon instant minced onion
1 tablespoon prepared horseradish
Salt
1 cup diced apple

Drain beets, reserving ½ cup of the liquid. Dissolve gelatin in hot water; add the ½ cup beet liquid, wine, lemon juice, onion, horseradish, and salt; chill. When mixture begins to thicken, fold in drained beets and diced apple. Pour into an oiled 1¼-quart ring mold; chill until firm. Unmold on crisp salad greens and serve with mayonnaise. *Serves 6.*

RAISIN PORT PIE

2 cups dark or golden raisins
1 cup water
$\frac{1}{2}$ cup Port
$\frac{1}{2}$ cup granulated sugar
2 tablespoons cornstarch
$\frac{1}{4}$ teaspoon salt
2 tablespoons butter or margarine
1 teaspoon grated lemon rind
$\frac{1}{4}$ cup lemon juice
Pastry for double 9-inch crust

Rinse and drain raisins. Add water and wine, and heat to boiling. Blend together sugar, cornstarch, and salt, add to raisin mixture, and cook, stirring until mixture boils thoroughly. Blend in butter, lemon rind and juice. Cool a few minutes. Turn into pastry-lined pie pan. Top with pastry. Bake in a very hot oven (450° F.) 10 minutes. Reduce heat to moderate (350° F.) and bake 30 to 40 minutes longer. Cool before cutting.

GLAZED CHERRY TARTLETTES

1½ tablespoons cornstarch
3 tablespoons sugar
Dash of cinnamon
Dash of salt
½ can syrup from canned red sour pitted
   cherries
½ cup Port
1 package (3-oz.) cream cheese
1 tablespoon milk
8 baked tart shells
3 cups drained canned red sour pitted cherries

Mix cornstarch, sugar, cinnamon, and salt in a
saucepan; gradually add cherry syrup and wine,
stirring until mixture is smooth. Stir over medium
heat until sauce is thickened and clear. Remove
from heat. Mash cream cheese with a fork; blend in
milk; spread mixture evenly over bottom of tart
shells. Place cherries in tart shells; pour sauce over
cherries. Chill thoroughly before serving. Serve
topped with whipped cream. *Serves 8.*

BLUEBERRY MERINGUE TART

1 quart fresh blueberries or 2 (10-oz.) packages
   frozen blueberries, thawed
1 cup sugar
$\frac{1}{2}$ teaspoon cinnamon
$\frac{1}{4}$ teaspoon salt
$\frac{1}{3}$ cup cornstarch
$\frac{2}{3}$ cup water
$\frac{2}{3}$ cup Port
2 tablespoons lemon juice
5 to 6 baked tart shells
2 egg whites

Crush 1 cup berries, reserve remaining whole ones.
Blend $\frac{1}{2}$ cup sugar, cinnamon, salt, and cornstarch
together in saucepan. Add crushed berries and
water. Heat and stir until mixture begins to simmer.
Blend in Port and lemon juice. Add whole berries;
cook gently until clear and thickened. Spoon into
baked pastry tart shells. Beat egg whites until
foamy. Add remaining $\frac{1}{2}$ cup sugar, a little at a time
and beating constantly until meringue stands in stiff
peaks. Spoon on top of tarts or swirl into peaks using
a pastry bag. Bake in a moderate oven (350° F.) until
meringue is very lightly browned, about 15 minutes.
Cool slightly before serving. *Serves 5–6.*

CHEESE AND APPLES PACIFICA

Red or golden Delicious apples
Small squares cream, Cheddar or Jack, and
  Roquefort cheeses
Small skewers
Salt
Port

Wash apples, dry and rub lightly with a little oil to give them a high gloss. Wipe off with paper toweling. Remove core of each apple to within an inch of bottom. Carefully cut apple into wedges to within an inch of bottom so apple retains its whole shape. Skewer a cube each of 3 kinds of cheese. Set one cheese skewer into center of each apple. Accompany with salt and glasses of mellow Port.

104

BAKED PEARS

1 tablespoon slivered orange rind
1 tablespoon slivered grapefruit rind
½ cup sugar
½ cup orange juice
6 whole cloves
Dash of salt
½ cup Port
6 fresh pears

To prepare orange and grapefruit rinds, cut orange or yellow part only from fruit, and sliver with sharp knife. Combine with sugar, orange juice, cloves, and salt, and boil 1 minute. Remove from heat and add wine. Cut pears in halves and remove cores. Place in shallow baking dish, cut side up, and pour wine syrup over them. Bake in moderate oven (350° F.) about 45 minutes, until tender, basting occasionally with syrup. Serve plain, or topped with sour cream and roasted slivered almonds. *Serves 6.*

GOURMET RHUBARB

1½ pounds rhubarb
⅔ to 1 cup sugar
¼ teaspoon salt
⅓ cup Port
1 teaspoon grated orange peel

Wash rhubarb and cut into ¾-inch slices. Place in baking dish with cover. Sprinkle sugar and salt over rhubarb; combine Port and orange peel and drizzle over all. Cover and bake in moderate oven (350° F.) for 35 to 40 minutes, just until tender. Chill before serving. (Note: Amount of sugar depends on one's taste for sweetness. Those who like tart rhubarb will want to use ⅔ cup sugar. For a sweet tooth, use as much as, but no more than, 1 cup.) *Serves 6.*

PORT AND TONIC

1 cup Port
2 cups quinine water (tonic mixer)
Crushed ice
Lemon wedges for garnish

Pour ¼ cup Port and ½ cup quinine water over crushed ice in each of 4 serving glasses. Stir lightly. Garnish with lemon wedges. *Serves 4.*

PORT FLIP

1 egg
⅓ cup Port
Ice, cracked or crushed

Combine all ingredients in covered container. Shake together until well blended. Strain into glass. *Serves 1.*

PORT SUNDAE SAUCE

¼ cup sugar
1 tablespoon cornstarch
1 cup Port
1 teaspoon lemon juice
2 teaspoons grated orange rind

Mix sugar and cornstarch. Add to Port in saucepan and cook, stirring frequently, until thickened and clear, about 5 minutes. Add lemon juice and orange rind. Chill. Serve over vanilla ice cream. *Serves 6.*

Muscatel

Like most of the sweeter wines, American Muscatel is produced primarily in the warm valleys of southern California, where the growing season extends long enough for the grapes to achieve maximum sugar content, and is warm enough to keep the acid content to a minimum. Most of the California Muscatel is produced from the Muscat of Alexandria grape. (Only a few winemakers produce a Muscat Frontignan to rival its French ancestor. This extremely sweet, very delicate dessert wine is in short supply, but it definitely is well worth the trouble of locating it.)

Muscatel almost singlehandedly gave wine an unsavory reputation in post-Prohibition America. Vineyards that had fallen to ruin during the dry years began grinding out quantities of inferior wines.

The sweeter they were, the less noticeable their poor quality. When America went on the glorious binge that followed Repeal, Scotch, bourbon, and gin were priced much higher than the average man could afford, for these were Depression years. So when a man who couldn't afford it really needed a drink, he turned to wine—in most cases, since it was most available, a cheap "muscatel"—and when he ended up unconscious on Skid Row with an empty wine bottle beside him, the term "wino" was born.

Despite all the slings and arrows, Muscatel remains a favored wine in America. Less heavy than Port or Cream Sherry, it is an excellent accompaniment to elaborate desserts. Yet it is versatile enough to complement the simple serving of fruit and cheese as well.

Cooking with Muscatel

Muscatel occupies a special place in cookery, and since it is basically a dessert wine, it obviously goes best in and with desserts, making the best better.

MUSCATEL

CHIFFON CREAM TARTS

1 envelope plain gelatin
½ cup Muscatel
2 eggs
½ cup sugar
1½ cups hot milk
¼ teaspoon salt
1 cup whipping cream
6 to 8 baked tart shells
1 tablespoon sugar
1 tablespoon Muscatel

Soften gelatin in ¼ cup Muscatel. Separate eggs. Beat yolks with ¼ cup of the sugar. Beat into hot milk. Cook and stir over hot water until mixture coats a spoon, about 20 minutes. Remove from heat. Add softened gelatin, stirring to dissolve. Stir in remaining ¼ cup wine. Chill until mixture begins to thicken. Beat egg whites with salt to soft peaks; gradually beat in remaining ¼ cup sugar. Beat ½ cup cream until stiff. Fold meringue and cream into chilled mixture. Spoon into tart shells. Chill until firm. When ready to serve, beat remaining ½ cup cream to soft peaks. Beat in 1 tablespoon sugar and 1 tablespoon Muscatel. Top each tart with a small puff of cream. Garnish with grated chocolate holly and a maraschino cherry. *Serves 6–8.*

AMBROSIA PIE

1 envelope unflavored gelatin
$\frac{1}{4}$ cup Muscatel
$\frac{1}{2}$ cup orange juice
1 tablespoon lemon juice
1 teaspoon each grated orange and lemon peel
1 cup sugar
Dash of salt
4 eggs, separated
1 cup flaked coconut
1 (9-inch) pastry shell, baked
$\frac{1}{2}$ cup heavy cream, whipped
Orange segments for garnishing

Soften gelatin in the wine. Combine orange juice,
lemon juice, orange peel, lemon peel, $\frac{1}{2}$ cup of the
sugar, salt, and egg yolks in top of double boiler;
cook, stirring, over boiling water for 5 to 10 minutes,
or until mixture thickens. Add softened gelatin; stir
until dissolved. Remove from heat. Beat egg whites
until stiff; gradually beat in remaining $\frac{1}{2}$ cup sugar;
fold into hot orange mixture; fold in $\frac{1}{2}$ cup coconut.
Pour into pie shell; chill until firm. Just before
serving, whip cream and spread over pie; sprinkle
with remaining coconut. Garnish with orange
segments.

APPLESAUCE MERINGUE

2 quarts peeled apple slices
$\frac{1}{2}$ cup sugar
$\frac{1}{8}$ teaspoon salt
$\frac{1}{3}$ cup Muscatel
2 tablespoons butter
1 tablespoon fresh lemon juice
$\frac{1}{2}$ teaspoon grated lemon rind
3 egg whites
6 tablespoons sugar

Combine all ingredients except egg whites and 6 tablespoons sugar. Cover and cook until apples are tender and like coarse applesauce. Turn into 10 by 6-inch baking dish. Prepare meringue by beating egg whites until stiff, adding sugar gradually during the beating. Spread over apples. Bake in a moderately hot oven (375° F.) until lightly browned on peaks, about 15 minutes. Serve warm. *Serves 6–8.*

114

CALIFORNIA PRUNE WHIP

1 cup cooked prunes
1 cup undiluted evaporated milk
1 (3-oz.) package lemon gelatin
³/₄ cup hot water
³/₄ cup Muscatel
2 tablespoons sugar
¹/₄ teaspoon salt

Cut prunes from pits into medium-sized pieces. Chill evaporated milk in ice tray. Dissolve gelatin in hot water; stir in Muscatel. Chill until partially set but not firm. Whip gelatin until foamy; beat evaporated milk to a moderately stiff peak; add sugar and salt. Combine gelatin and cream mixture, and blend together; add prunes and continue beating until blended. Chill 1 hour or longer before serving. *Serves 8–10.*

GLAZED ORANGES SUPREME

6 large oranges
$1/4$ cup orange juice
4 thin lemon slices
Pinch of salt
$1/2$ cup Muscatel
$1^1/_2$ cups sugar
Firm vanilla ice cream
Pound or sponge cake slices

Peel and segment oranges. Combine orange juice,
lemon slices, salt, wine, and sugar in a saucepan.
Bring to a boil and simmer about 20 minutes or
until a thin thread forms. Add orange segments and
remove from heat. Serve ice cream on cake slices and
spoon warm or cold glazed oranges and sauce over
top. *Serves 6.*

MUSCATEL FIG BARS

1 cup dried figs
$\frac{1}{3}$ cup Muscatel
$\frac{1}{2}$ cup butter or margarine
$\frac{2}{3}$ cup brown sugar (packed)
1 egg, beaten
2 cups sifted all-purpose flour
$1\frac{1}{2}$ teaspoons baking powder
$\frac{1}{2}$ teaspoon salt
$\frac{1}{2}$ teaspoon nutmeg
$\frac{1}{2}$ cup milk
Wine Glaze (recipe below)
$\frac{1}{3}$ cup sliced almonds or Brazil nuts

Rinse and drain figs; clip off stems and cut figs into small pieces. Combine figs and wine and let stand about $\frac{1}{2}$ hour. Cream butter, sugar, and egg until fluffy. Sift flour, baking powder, salt, and nutmeg together. Add to creamed mixture alternately with milk. Stir in fig mixture. Turn into a greased shallow oblong pan about 11-by-15 inches; spread batter evenly in pan. Bake in moderately hot oven (375° F.) about 20 to 25 minutes. Remove from oven, cool in pan. When cold spread with Wine Glaze; sprinkle with nuts. Cut into small bars. *Makes 30–40 bars.*

Wine Glaze: Blend together 1 tablespoon soft butter or margarine, $1\frac{1}{2}$ cups sifted powdered sugar, and 2 tablespoons Muscatel or Sherry until smooth.

APRICOT-RAISIN CONSERVE

1/2 cup dried apricots
1 1/2 cups dark seedless raisins
2 cups water
1 cup brown sugar (packed)
1/4 cup fresh lemon juice
1/2 cup Muscatel

Rinse apricots and raisins; drain. Simmer in water
until tender — about 20 minutes. Add brown sugar
and lemon juice; cook until thick. Cool to lukewarm;
stir in wine. Conserve may be served at once or
sealed in sterilized jars. *Makes about 1 1/2 pints.*

APPLE-RAISIN CONSERVE

1 cup dark or golden raisins
4 cups chopped, peeled Washington apples
1/3 cup lemon juice
1/3 cup water
3 cups sugar
1 tablespoon grated orange rind
1/4 teaspoon cinnamon
1/4 teaspoon nutmeg
1/2 cup coarsely-chopped walnuts
1/4 cup Muscatel

Combine raisins, apples, lemon juice, water and
sugar in a large saucepan. Cook until apples are
transparent and mixture is thick — about 30 minutes.
Add orange rind and spices. Cool to lukewarm; stir
in nuts and wine. Let stand until cold and thick
before serving, or pour into sterilized jars and seal.
Makes about 1 quart.

118

"MARSHCATEL" SALAD DRESSING

1 cup bottled marshmallow whip
$\frac{1}{4}$ cup mayonnaise
$\frac{1}{4}$ cup lemon juice
2 tablespoons Muscatel
Grated peel of 1 lemon
Grated peel of 1 orange
$\frac{1}{4}$ teaspoon dry mustard
$\frac{1}{8}$ teaspoon salt
2 egg whites

Combine marshmallow whip, mayonnaise, lemon juice, Muscatel, lemon and orange peels, mustard, and salt; beat until well blended; chill. Just before serving, beat egg whites until stiff and gently fold into marshmallow mixture. Serve with fruit salads. *Makes 3 cups.*

HOLIDAY ANGEL DESSERT

⅓ cup cornstarch
¾ cup sugar
½ teaspoon salt
1 cup orange juice
1 tablespoon lemon juice
2 eggs
½ cup Muscatel
2 tablespoons brandy
1½ cups whipping cream
1 baked 10-inch custard or plain angel food
   cake
½ cup red currant jelly
1 (3½-oz.) can flaked coconut

Blend cornstarch, sugar and salt together; stir into
orange juice. Cook and stir until mixture thickens,
10 to 15 minutes. Beat eggs; blend a little of the hot
mixture into eggs, then stir back into larger portion
of filling. Add wine and brandy. Cook 2 or 3 minutes
longer; beat smooth. Cool, then chill. Fold cold
orange-wine filling into stiffly beaten cream. Cut
cake crosswise into 3 (or you can make 4) layers.
Spread one cut side of each layer with currant jelly,
beaten with a fork for easy spreading. Then put
layers together with some of the creamy orange-wine
filling. Spread remaining filling over top and sides of
cake. Sprinkle coconut over top and sides. Chill
until ready to serve. Garnish with maraschino
cherries or candied cherries and green spearmint
candy leaves. (Split leaves in half to make thin
leaves.) *Serves 12.*

INCEMEAT TURNOVER WITH WINE AUCE

cups sifted all-purpose flour
teaspoon salt
 cup shortening
to 5 tablespoons orange juice
cups mincemeat
ine Sauce

ft flour and salt into mixing bowl. Cut in
ortening. Add orange juice to make stiff dough.
ape into a ball. Roll out on floured board to an
long, about 10 × 15-inches. Spread mincemeat
ong front half of pastry strip. Bring back pastry
rward over mincemeat; press all edges of pastry
mly together. Turn pastry edges in, slightly, to
al; flute if desired. Place turnover on baking sheet.
ick top with tines of fork; sprinkle with sugar,
desired. Bake in a hot oven (425° F.) for 15 to 20
inutes or until rich golden brown. Cool slightly;
t into strips and serve with Wine Sauce. *Makes 6 to 8 servings*

ine Sauce:

cup sugar
w grains salt
tablespoon cornstarch
cup orange juice
cup Muscatel
easpoon grated orange rind

end all ingredients together. Bring
 a boil, lower heat and simmer about 5 minutes.
rve warm.

121

GINGERBREAD-PEAR PUDDING

$\frac{1}{4}$ cup butter or margarine
$\frac{1}{2}$ cup brown sugar (packed)
$\frac{1}{4}$ cup Muscatel
2 large fresh pears (about 2 cups sliced) or
   1 (No. $2\frac{1}{2}$ can) canned pears, drained and
   sliced
1 ($14\frac{1}{2}$-oz.) package gingerbread mix
$\frac{1}{3}$ cup Muscatel
$\frac{2}{3}$ cup water
Whipped cream for topping

Melt butter in the bottom of a 9-inch square pan.
Blend in sugar and $\frac{1}{4}$ cup Muscatel. Arrange pear
slices, fresh or canned, in rows in pan mixture. Beat
gingerbread mix, $\frac{1}{3}$ cup Muscatel and water
together vigorously until blended. Carefully spoon
over pears. Bake in a moderately hot oven (350° F.)
for 30 to 35 minutes. Cut into squares (or spoon
out into serving dishes). Serve warm topped with
whipped cream. *Makes 9 squares.*

122

BROWN SUGAR PUDDING SAUCE

½ cup brown sugar (packed)
1 tablespoon cornstarch
⅛ teaspoon salt
½ cup water
¼ cup finely-chopped walnuts
1 tablespoon grated orange rind
2 tablespoons butter or margarine
¼ cup Muscatel

Combine sugar, cornstarch and salt in a heavy saucepan. Add water; cook until mixture is thick and clear. Stir in walnuts, orange rind, butter and wine. Serve warm over steamed or cottage pudding. *Makes 1¼ cups.*

Angelica

While the mission grape — the first *vinifera* variety
to be successfully grown in the New World — is today
virtually limited to the production of sacramental
wines, it is still the principal grape used in the
golden Angelica wine, said to be named for the city
of Los Angeles. One of the sweetest of all dessert
wines, Angelica is produced only in California and
only by a few vintners. It is very rarely found
outside of its native state.

Madeira

Madeira is a lush, picturesque island in the Atlantic
just off Gibraltar. When Europeans discovered it in
the fifteenth century, they decided it would make
fine wine grape country and proceeded to defoliate
the tiny paradise by means of a gigantic forest fire.
(Fortunately they allowed enough green to grow
back so that today the island looks like an exquisite
emerald dropped almost by accident into the gray
Atlantic.) The wood ash from the fire and the
indigenous volcanic soil provided the ideal
combination for growing sweet wine grapes.

Madeira from Madeira remains unmatched, and
though some American wineries have made an
attempt to duplicate this unique wine, their products
bear little resemblance to the original.

Cooking with Madeira

Madeira is almost as versatile as Sherry in cooking,
lending a smokey flavor and special elegance to
light meats, such as veal and ham, and all fowl.
In many of the recipes that call for Sherry, Madeira
may be substituted for a taste variation.

MADEIRA

CHEESE BON-BONS

1 (8-oz.) package cream cheese
2 tablespoons blue cheese, crumbled
2 to 3 tablespoons Madeira
$\frac{1}{8}$ teaspoon curry powder (if you like curry, use
    up to $\frac{1}{4}$ teaspoon)
Bon-Bon coating

Blend all ingredients except Bon-Bon coating until
smooth. Cover and chill at least 4 hours to firm
mixture and mellow flavors. Roll into small balls,
about an inch in diameter. Coat each Bon-Bon with
one of the following: finely chopped peanuts; chopped
parsley, chives, or fresh mint; toasted sesame seeds;
caraway seeds; dried dill; paprika. Makes about
$1\frac{1}{2}$ dozen.

VEAL MADEIRAN

1½ pounds veal scaloppine
Flour, seasoned with salt and pepper
Butter
½ pound fresh mushrooms, sliced
¾ cup Madeira

Dredge veal in seasoned flour and sauté in butter until just browned. Lightly sauté mushrooms in butter; add to veal. Pour Madeira over veal and mushrooms and stir sauce as it heats – it will thicken very slightly. Serve immediately, pouring sauce over each serving. *Serves 4.*

CHICKEN CITRON

2 broiler-fryer chickens, halved
Salt and pepper
2 tablespoons lemon juice
3 tablespoons melted butter
½ cup Madeira
1 cup strained orange juice

Sprinkle cavity of chickens with salt and pepper.
Arrange cut side down on broiling platter or pan.
Sprinkle lemon juice over chicken; drizzle on butter;
sprinkle with salt and pepper. Broil about 5 inches
from heat until chickens begin to take on color. Pour
on Madeira and orange juice. Cover tightly with foil.
Lower heat to moderately hot (375° F.). Bake until
tender, 25 to 30 minutes. Drain off pan liquid; skim
off any excess fat. Boil rapidly to reduce sauce about
½ (should be slightly thickened). Spoon over chicken
when served. *Serves 4.*

128

SWISS STEAK MADEIRA

½ cup flour
Salt and pepper
2 pounds round steak, cut 1 inch thick
3 tablespoons bacon drippings or other fat
1 medium-size onion, chopped
1 clove garlic, chopped (optional)
1 cup chopped celery
1 (8-oz.) can tomato sauce
½ cup Madeira
1 (8-oz.) can mushroom stems and pieces
  (undrained)

Mix flour with salt and pepper. Pound mixture into
steak on both sides, using a wooden mallet. Cut
steak into serving-size portions. Heat bacon drippings
in a large, heavy skillet or a Dutch oven; brown
pieces of steak nicely on both sides. Add all
remaining ingredients; season with salt and pepper.
Cover and bake in a moderate oven (350° F.) about
1½ hours, or until steak is tender. Turn and baste
steak occasionally, and add a little water if needed
to keep gravy from becoming too thick. *Serves 6.*

CALIFORNIA RANCHO CASSEROLE

2 tablespoons salad oil
1 pound ground beef
½ cup chopped onion
1 clove garlic, chopped (optional)
1 cup uncooked rice
1 cup sliced ripe olives
1 (4-oz.) can mushroom stems and pieces
1 (No. 303) can tomatoes
½ cup Madeira
Salt and pepper
1 cup grated Cheddar cheese
2 tablespoons chopped parsley
Paprika

Heat oil in a large, heavy skillet or a Dutch oven;
sauté beef, onion, and garlic until meat is no longer
red, stirring with a fork to separate meat into small
bits. Add rice, olives, undrained mushrooms,
tomatoes, wine, salt, and pepper. Mix well; bring to a
boil; pour into a 2-quart casserole. Cover and bake
in a moderately hot oven (375° F.) for 30 minutes.
Uncover; with a fork, gently stir in cheese. Cover
and continue baking 15 minutes. Uncover; stir
gently again. Sprinkle with parsley and paprika,
and serve. *Serves 6.*

AMBROSIA

2 cups fresh orange sections (3 to 4 oranges)
1 banana
$\frac{1}{4}$ cup powdered sugar
$\frac{1}{8}$ teaspoon cinnamon
$\frac{1}{2}$ cup flaked coconut
$\frac{1}{4}$ cup Madeira

Prepare orange sections and slice banana. Mix
together sugar and cinnamon. Arrange layers of
fruits and coconut in serving bowl, sprinkling each
layer of fruit with some of the sugar mixture. Pour
Madeira over all. Cover and chill for several hours
before serving. *Serves 4.*

THE FLAVORED WINES

"Then a smile and a glass and a toast and a cheer,
For all the good wine, and we've some of it here."
— Oliver Wendell Holmes

Among the flavored wines made in America, two
stand out because of their quality and popularity:
Dubonnet and Vermouth.

Dubonnet

Once exclusively French, Dubonnet is now almost
exclusively American. The red — Dubonnet *Rouge* —
is sweet; the white — Dubonnet *Blonde* — is lighter
and slightly drier. Both are pleasantly flavored with
bitter bark and quinine. Their sweetness comes from
blending with a little dessert wine. Served on the
rocks, or with club soda for a tall drink, they make
ideal apéritifs. A slice of lemon, or a twist, goes
especially well with the *Rouge.*

The Vermouths

Vermouth gained its initial success in America
largely because of its mixing ability in such favorites
as the Dry Martini, the Manhattan, the Rob Roy.
As Martinis got drier and drier, less and less
Vermouth was used in them, but the increasing
popularity of these cocktails kept the demand for
Vermouth rising. Today, however, more and more
people are discovering how pleasant the Vermouths
can be — on their own, on the rocks with a twist of
lemon, or with a splash of soda (one of the many
"spritzers" that are gaining favor). Still another
combination is the half-and-half — made from equal
parts of sweet and dry Vermouths. Some winemakers
are now bottling their own blends of half-and-half,
with growing success.

133

Vermouth is essentially an aromatic, fortified wine to which herbs and spices have been added to produce a subtle complexity of flavors. While the concept of adding herbs to wines dates back to Greek and Roman times, the actual name "Vermouth" stems from the early Teutons who added the shrub wormwood — *wermut* in German — to wine. When these wines began to achieve popularity in Italy and France in the late eighteenth century, the name became Vermouth.

All Vermouth begins as a neutral white wine, fermented in the usual way and then brought up to about 18 percent alcohol by adding neutral wine brandy. Up to this point, the process of making both dry and sweet Vermouths is the same.

Dry Vermouth   For dry Vermouths, a blend of herbs is steeped in the fortified wine base, much as tea leaves are steeped in hot water. A Vermouth formula may contain as few as ten, as many as 100 herbs, leaves, roots, flowers, twigs, barks — ranging from angostura and angelica to yarrow and zedoary. After a time, the herb mixture is removed and the wine allowed to rest while the various flavors mingle and balance. No one herb should dominate. Since each winemaker has his own recipe for Vermouth, you will find variations—not only in flavor, but color—the driest are so pale as to seem clear, those with even a trace of sweetness may appear golden.

Sweet Vermouth   The sweet Vermouths are treated somewhat differently. After the initial fermentation and the addition of brandy, the base wine is blended with a sweeter dessert wine such as Angelica, Port, or Muscatel. Although these wines help to give sweet Vermouth its characteristic amber color, small amounts of caramel are also added to deepen it. Only then is the wine steeped in aromatic herbs (quinine gives it the slight bitterness that is characteristic) and laid to rest until the desired balance of flavors is achieved.

Dry Vermouth is traditionally called French, the sweet, Italian—no matter where they are made. However, Italy and some of the other Mediterranean countries have been producing a semi-sweet white Vermouth called Bianca that is lighter-bodied and less pungent than either the classic dry or sweet. Some of this delightful wine is now being imported into the United States; hopefully, American vintners will rise to the challenge and begin producing it in this country.

Cooking with Vermouth

There is no question that Vermouth is still used primarily in cocktails, but creative cooks are discovering that this wine can be a virtual "liquid herb" in the home kitchen.

VERMOUTH

CLAM 'N OYSTER STEW

1 (8-oz.) can oysters
1 (7-oz.) can minced clams
1½ cups light cream
¼ cup dry Vermouth
½ teaspoon instant minced onion
1 tablespoon butter or margarine
Salt and pepper

Combine oysters and clams with their liquor with all remaining ingredients, seasoning to taste with salt and pepper. Heat slowly until piping hot.
Serves 4.

SOLE MARJORIE

6 slices fillet of sole (about 2 pounds)
1½ teaspoons seasoned salt
⅛ teaspoon dried dill
1 tablespoon finely chopped parsley
½ cup dry Vermouth
3 tablespoons tarragon or shallot wine vinegar
¼ cup water
1½ teaspoons cornstarch
2 teaspoons water
2 tablespoons butter
⅛ teaspoon paprika
3 cups hot cooked peas
Sour Cream Sauce (recipe below)

Place slices of sole in a shallow casserole. Sprinkle
with salt, dill, and parsley. Pour on Vermouth and
vinegar. Cover and marinate in refrigerator 1 hour.
Drain off and save marinade. Roll up each fillet like
a jelly roll; skewer with a toothpick. Pour marinade
and ¼ cup water into a medium-small skillet. Heat
to simmering; place fish rolls in hot liquid. Simmer
gently, turning carefully or basting until fish is
cooked, about 5 or 6 minutes. Remove sole and keep
hot. Blend cornstarch with 2 teaspoons water. Stir
into liquid in pan; add butter and paprika. Cook
and stir until sauce boils and thickens. Add a little
additional salt, if necessary. Set fish rolls upright
in a serving dish. Spoon hot cooked peas around
rolls; spoon sauce over all. Serve with Sour Cream
Sauce, if desired. *Serves 6.*

Sour Cream Sauce: Stir together ½ cup dairy sour
cream, ½ cup mayonnaise, 1 tablespoon catsup,
¼ cup sweet pickle relish (drained), ¼ teaspoon
grated lemon rind, and 1 teaspoon lemon juice. Chill
before serving with sole. Makes about 1 cup.

SESAME CHICKEN

6 large chicken breasts
$\frac{1}{2}$ cup dry Vermouth
1 tablespoon soy sauce
$\frac{1}{2}$ teaspoon powdered ginger
$\frac{1}{2}$ pound fresh mushrooms
6 green onions
1 large firm, ripe tomato
1 tablespoon butter
1 tablespoon shortening or oil
$\frac{1}{2}$ teaspoon garlic salt
$\frac{1}{2}$ cup chicken broth
2 teaspoons cornstarch
1 tablespoon dry Vermouth
1 tablespoon toasted sesame seeds

Have butcher bone chicken (or remove bones with thin-bladed sharp knife); remove skin. Combine the $\frac{1}{2}$ cup Vermouth, soy sauce, and ginger. Pour over chicken and let stand 1 hour. Meanwhile, trim stems and cut mushrooms in half. Trim and cut onions in 1-inch diagonal strips; cut tomato into small wedges. Drain chicken well, reserving marinade. Heat butter and shortening in a skillet. Add chicken and brown lightly on both sides. Sprinkle with garlic salt. Add mushrooms, onions, reserved marinade, and chicken broth. Cover and simmer until tender, about 15 minutes. Blend cornstarch with the 1 tablespoon Vermouth. Stir into pan liquid. Add tomato and cook a few minutes longer until sauce is thickened and clear. Sprinkle with sesame seeds. *Serves 6.*

140

BAKED SOLE VERMOUTH

1 pound fillet of sole
Salt
2 green onions
½ cup dry Vermouth
1 tablespoon butter or margarine
1 tablespoon flour
Dash of cayenne pepper
¼ cup sliced ripe olives
1 tablespoon chopped parsley
2 teaspoons lemon juice

Sprinkle fish with salt and arrange in greased
shallow baking dish. Chop onions and sprinkle over
fish. Add wine and bake in hot oven (400° F.) for
15 minutes. Melt butter and blend in flour, cayenne,
and salt to taste. Drain wine from fish into butter
and flour mixture, and cook and stir over hot water
until thickened. Add olives, parsley, and lemon
juice. Pour sauce over fish. *Serves 4.*

GOLDEN COCKTAIL

1 pint chilled apple juice
1 cup dry Vermouth
Twist of lemon peel

Combine apple juice and Vermouth, and chill thoroughly. Serve with a twist of lemon peel in each glass. *Makes 1½ pints.*

PINEAPPLE FROST

1 can (6-oz.) frozen pineapple juice concentrate
4 cups crushed ice
2 cups dry Vermouth

Combine all ingredients in blender jar and blend about 10 seconds, until frosty. *6 servings.*

VERMOUTH AND ORANGE JUICE

2 oz. (¼ cup) dry Vermouth
½ cup orange juice
1 teaspoon lime juice
Sparkling water

Combine Vermouth, orange juice and lime juice in tall glass half filled with ice cubes. Fill glass with sparkling water. *One serving.*

VERMOUTH LIVER PATÉ

1 pound chicken livers
1 teaspoon garlic salt
$\frac{1}{2}$ teaspoon powdered rosemary
$\frac{3}{4}$ cup dry Vermouth
$\frac{1}{2}$ teaspoon paprika
1 tablespoon flour
$\frac{1}{4}$ cup butter

Rinse and drain chicken livers. Dredge with seasonings mixed with flour. Sauté to a rich golden brown in melted butter. Add $\frac{1}{2}$ cup Vermouth; cover and simmer until livers are tender. Remove from heat, add remaining Vermouth and cool. Puree or blend in an electric blender until smooth. Cover and refrigerate several hours to mellow flavors. *Makes about 2 cups.*

Other Flavored Wines

In his search for the ultimate beverage, man has for centuries been flavoring his wines with everything from resin (the Greek *retsina*), to honey (the Romans), to woodruff, an herb used by the Germans to flavor new wine for enjoyment at their famous May Wine festivals. In recent years, American vintners have developed a range of special flavored wines unmatched anywhere, anytime. They come in just about every color and may be flavored with one or more fruit juices, berries, and extracts such as vanilla, cocoa, and coffee. Such spices as cinnamon go into the new *aprés-ski* wines. Designed to be served hot, these wines can be turned into a quite passable *glügg* by adding a shot of vodka to each cup. Obviously, these wines, which bear names as fanciful as their flavors, are not for the purist, and they make no pretensions. But taken for what they are—perhaps it's best to think of them as wine *drinks*—they can be tasty and refreshing.

Coffee-flavored wine seems to be currently garnering more attention than the rest. At one time it was produced only by one of the smaller vineyards in Southern California; now several of the best known wineries are marketing it. A personal favorite, this

144

is a marvelous after-dinner drink, and obviously a perfect companion for coffee. Less alcoholic than the coffee liqueur, Kahlúa, it has the same sweet, rich flavor and imparts the same luxurious sense of well-being.

Coffee wine has a natural affinity to food. Next time you're making devil's food cake, try replacing two ounces of the liquid with a coffee-flavored wine. Pour it over vanilla ice cream. And by all means try this simple recipe, so named to honor the fact that California not only originated Irish Coffee (it was invented at the Buena Vista Cafe in San Francisco) but gave us coffee wine as a bonus.

CALIFORNIA COFFEE

1 cup strong black coffee
1½ ounces coffee wine (about a shot glass full)
Whipped cream

Pour the wine into the coffee and top with cold whipped cream.

SPARKLING WINES

"In water one sees one's own face; but in wine, one beholds the heart of another."

—Old French Proverb

Even while America took its own good time in recognizing wine as part of the good life on a daily basis, sparkling wines were the accepted drink for all festive occasions. No wedding, no christening, no New Year's Eve would have been complete without a toast in the bubbly. And because the excellent American Champagnes and Sparkling Burgundies are so modestly priced, people have added birthdays, job promotions, anniversaries, and a host of other celebrations to the list of occasions on which to enjoy them. Sparkling wines are more expensive than most still wines for two very good reasons. Our tax laws put an added levy on sparkling wines, and in the making of these wines there is an extra process which is exacting and time-consuming.

Champagne

The initial steps in making Champagne, whether white, pink, or red (Sparkling Burgundy is, in fact, a red Champagne), are the same as for still wines. Only after the desired blending has been performed and the wine is ready for bottling does the actual Champagne-making process begin.

In the traditional method, the wine is given a dosage of yeast culture and sweetening ingredients. It is then bottled and given a temporary cap that resembles those found on soda and beer bottles. The bottles are placed in racks, necks pointed downward at a sharp angle, the bottoms of the bottles facing out. A white stripe is painted on the bottom of each bottle.

This is not decoration. Each day, for the several weeks during which a *second fermentation* is taking place in the bottle, the bottle is given a quarter-turn, clockwise, the stripe indicating just how much to turn it. This process is called *riddling*, and it requires great dexterity of the wrists. (Because of the carbon dioxide pressure building up in the bottles, riddlers usually wear masks similar to those used by welders to avoid injury in case of an exploding bottle.)

During this second fermentation, sediment is thrown. The riddling keeps it from collecting along the sides of the bottle, while the tilt of the bottle forces the sediment down into the neck.

When the fermentation period is ended, the bottles are plunged neck down into a freezing brine solution. The sediment-filled part freezes solid. The bottles are then ready for *dégorgement,* or disgorging. The cap is removed and the pressure in the wine forces the frozen sediment to shoot out of the bottle. Then, before too much air can enter or any of the bubbles dissipate, some older wine is added to replace what was lost. A bit of brandy is also added to stabilize the wine, as well as another dosage that varies in sweetness, according to whether the wine is to be very dry, dry, or slightly sweet. The bottles are then given their final closure — the traditional fat and tapered champagne cork with its metal wire twisted around the neck of the bottle to keep it in place.

148

This is the classic way of making Champagne, and the best American Champagnes, both California and New York, are produced this way. However, many producers make a satisfying sparkling wine by the *bulk,* or *Charmat,* process, by which the second fermentation takes place in a vat which is sealed to prevent the carbon dioxide bubbles from escaping. When the fermentation has been completed, the wine is filtered to remove the sediment and bottled in the traditional way.

One way to tell whether a sparkling wine has been made in the classic manner is by the price. Another way is by the label on the bottle. Bulk process Champagnes are by far the least expensive and the labels carry the notation "Bulk process." The finest — and most expensive — champagnes will read, "Naturally fermented in this bottle." The "this" in the phrase is important, for it indicates that the Champagne was produced by the *dégorgement* method, which means that the Champagne retains a maximum of sparkle. (The bottle will probably have traces of the white riddling stripe on the bottom.) Other Champagnes may carry the notation "Naturally fermented in the bottle." This means that while the secondary fermentation did indeed take place in the bottle, *dégorgement* was not used. Instead, in a process called the *transfer method,* the fermented wine was removed from that bottle, passed through a filter to remove the sediment, and then rebottled. Many high quality American Champagnes are produced in this way. Their prices may range from moderate (though seldom as little as bulk process wines) to as high as any of those in which *dégorgement* was used.

Of course, method alone will not determine the quality of Champagne, Pink Champagne, or Sparkling Burgundy. The original wines chosen to become sparkling are a big factor, for an inferior still wine will produce an inferior Champagne. So, as always, the deciding elements are the grapes and the winemaker's skill.

Virtually all sparkling wines are blends. The white Champagnes are usually made up of Pino Chardonnay, White Pinot, and Pinot Noir, fermented without the skins so that they impart no color, but give a degree of body and fullness lacking in the white grapes. The best Pink Champagnes originate as Rosé, and the finer the original wine, the finer the Champagne. Sparkling Burgundy is a blend of several red wines; obviously, the more predominate the superb Pinot Noir, the better the finished product.

Eastern wineries have become justly famous for excellent Champagnes and Sparkling Burgundies, made by blending the starter wine from Eastern hybrids with *Vitis vinifera* wines from California. The characteristic grape flavor tends to disappear in the double fermentation, and, whereas Eastern still wines have yet to catch the fancy of the ultimate connoisseur, New York State Champagnes are ranked with the world's finest.

150

American Champagnes range from very dry to slightly sweet in this order: *Brut* — the driest; *Extra Dry; Dry* — some dry Champagnes are labeled *Sec;* and *Demi-Sec* — indicating a degree of sweetness. *Brut* is the choice of the experts, but most of this country's Champagne afficionados prefer *Extra Dry.*

The Pink Champagnes and Sparkling Burgundies are deliberately blended to appeal to America's slightly sweet taste. The pinks can range from excellent to cloying; the Sparkling Burgundies are more reliably on the dry side.

Cooking with Champagne

Because Champagne bubbles are so elusive and fragile, this wine is seldom used in the preparation of hot foods. These superb dishes are exceptions.

CHAMPAGNE

ELEGANT CHICKEN

2 frying chickens (2 to 2½ pounds each)
½ cup butter
¼ cup sifted flour
2 teaspoons seasoned salt
⅛ teaspoon pepper
½ teaspoon ground ginger
2 tablespoons brown sugar
½ cup Sauterne, Chablis, or other white dinner
    wine
1 cup orange juice
½ cup chicken broth
2 oranges, cut in slices
1 cup Champagne

Wash chicken pieces and dry with paper toweling.
Melt butter over low heat in a heavy skillet. Brown
chicken slowly on all sides. Remove from pan.
Blend flour, seasoned salt, pepper, ginger, and brown
sugar into pan drippings. Slowly stir in white dinner
wine, orange juice, and broth. Cook and stir until
sauce boils and thickens. Remove from heat, add
chicken pieces, cover and cool. Refrigerate until
about 1 hour before time to serve. Slowly reheat
contents of pan to simmering. Cook, covered, until
chicken is tender, about 25 to 30 minutes. Add
orange slices and Champagne. Continue cooking 10
to 15 minutes longer. Spoon sauce over each serving.
Serves 6.

CHOUCROUTE GARNIE

2 quarts sauerkraut
4 small boiling onions
12 whole cloves
1 bay leaf
8 juniper berries
1 teaspoon peppercorns
1 sprig thyme or ½ teaspoon thyme leaves
1 (⅘-qt.) bottle Sauterne
1 (⅘-pt.) bottle Champagne
6 smoked pork chops or thick slices smoked
   pork loin
2 cooking apples
1½ pounds sausages (Polish sausage ring, Swiss
   sausage, frankfurters, or garlic sausages)

Drain sauerkraut, and rinse lightly. Stud onions
with cloves. Tie bay leaf, juniper berries, peppercorns, and thyme in square of cheesecloth. Place in
large kettle with onions and sauerkraut, and add
Sauterne. Cover and simmer 1 hour. Meanwhile
place Champagne bottle in warm water. After
sauerkraut has cooked an hour, add pork chops and
cook 45 minutes longer. Core and slice apples. Add
to kettle, and cook 5 minutes, then add sausages,
and simmer 10 minutes to heat through. Arrange
sauerkraut and meats on heated platter, with
warmed Champagne bottle in center. Carry to the
table, open Champagne, and let it foam over
sauerkraut and sausages. (Note: A pinch of sugar
dropped into the Champagne bottle will make it
foam up vigorously. Change water occasionally, to
insure having contents of bottle warm when it is
opened.) *Serves 6–8.*

BRIDE AND GROOM PUNCH

1 cup sugar
2 cups water
Rind of 2 oranges, cut in strips
Rind of 2 lemons, cut in strips
Several sprigs fresh mint
2 (⅘-qt.) bottles Sauterne or other white dinner
  wine
2 (6-oz.) cans frozen orange juice concentrate
½ cup lemon juice
1 large bottle Champagne

Combine sugar, water, orange rinds, lemon rinds,
and mint in a saucepan. Bring to a boil, stirring
until sugar is dissolved; simmer 5 minutes. Remove
from heat. Cool thoroughly, then strain. Combine
this syrup with the wine, frozen orange juice
concentrate, and lemon juice in a punch bowl. Add
a block of ice or a try of ice cubes, then pour in
Champagne. Serve at once. *Makes 30 3-ounce
servings.*

APRICOT TINGLE

6 to 8 whole canned apricots
6 to 8 ounces Cream Sherry, chilled
1 (⁴/₅-quart) bottle Champagne, chilled

Drain apricots and freeze fruit. Place frozen apricots
in tulip glasses, 1 apricot to each glass. Add 1 ounce
Sherry to each and fill with chilled Champagne.
Serves 6–8.

GOLDEN WEDDING PUNCH

1 (6-oz.) can frozen orange juice concentrate
1 cup lemon juice
1 (No. 2) can pineapple juice
1 cup sugar
1 (⁴/₅-qt.) bottle Sauterne or other white dinner
wine, chilled
2 large bottled Champagne, chilled

Mix fruit juices and sugar; stir to dissolve sugar.
Cover; chill in refrigerator several hours. Just before
serving, pour mixture over block of ice in punch
bowl. Add Sauterne and Champagne. Serve at once.
Punch may be garnished with orange slices,
maraschino cherries, or strawberries, if desired.
Makes 35 3-ounce servings.

CHAMPAGNE SODAS

Champagne
Pineapple sundae sauce or partially defrosted
  frozen raspberries
Pineapple or lemon sherbet

Chill Champagne. Spoon 1 tablespoon sundae sauce
(or 2 tablespoons raspberries) into 6- or 8-ounce
glasses. Add 1 small scoop sherbet to each glass and
stir to partially blend. Add another scoop sherbet
and fill glass with well-chilled Champagne.

SPARKLING FRUIT COBBLER

1 qt. mixed firm ripe fruit (melon balls, pitted
  cherries, grapes, sliced peaches are good
  choices)
1 ($\frac{4}{5}$-qt.) bottle sweet Sauterne or light sweet
  Muscat wine
1 chilled ($\frac{4}{5}$-qt. bottle) Champagne

Combine fruits and sweet Sauterne. Cover and chill
well several hours. When ready to serve, spoon into
large compotes or small brandy snifters. Pour on
Champagne. *Serves 8.*

CHAMPAGNE FRUIT SAUCE

1 cup pineapple-grapefruit juice
$\frac{1}{2}$ cup orange juice
2 tablespoons lemon juice
$\frac{1}{2}$ teaspoon grated orange rind
3 tablespoons cornstarch
$\frac{1}{8}$ teaspoon salt
1 cup Champagne

Stir fruit juices, orange rind, cornstarch and salt together in saucepan until blended. Cook and stir until sauce boils and thickens. Remove from heat; cool 5 minutes. Stir in Champagne just before serving. *Makes about 2½ cups.*

SPICED PEACH CHAMPAGNE CUP

1 (1-lb. 14-oz.) can whole spiced peaches
1 bottle (26 ounces) chilled Champagne
6 slices lime

Chill peaches in can. Spoon about 3 tablespoons spiced syrup into each 6 or 8-oz. glass. Place spiced peach in each and fill glass with Champagne (about $\frac{1}{3}$ cup). Garnish with lime slice, serve with a spoon. *Serves 6.*

Cold Duck

"Pop wines—so called because of their popularity
with the young crowd (and, according to their critics,
their similarity to soda pop)—are the new phenomena
in the wine industry. Some may scoff, but in the
past few years they have acquired some 15 percent
of wine sales.

Probably the best known is Cold Duck, a sparkling
wine concoction that has been largely responsible
for doubling the quantity of sparkling wine
consumed in this country over the past two years.
Experts are a bit hazy about the ancestry of Cold
Duck, but the favorite story is that it originated a
century or so ago in Germany, where after a party,
the leftover wines were mixed together and some
Champagne added to spark up the beverage, which
was called *kalte ente*—"cold end." Somehow this
phrase evolved into something that sounded in
English like "cold duck." The name stuck, though
it has about as much resemblance to *Kalte ente* as
the beverage we know has to those "cold ends."

The Cold Duck we buy is a blend of slightly sweet
Champagne and Sparkling Burgundy, and is much

less expensive than either Champagne or Sparkling Burgundy alone. A fun, festive drink, very much suited to the mood and pocketbook of the younger generation, it is produced by many vintners in California and New York — with some of them adding adjectives to the name to distinguish their particular products: *Extra* Cold Duck, for example, or *Very* Cold Duck. These embellishments would tend to show a sense of humor which reinforces the fact that these are not wines to be taken seriously, but are fun wines that can give a great deal of pleasure when accepted for what they are.

The instant success of Cold Duck was probably what inspired the flood of popularly priced wines and wine drinks, most of them marketed under special names belonging to individual wineries. There are the spritzer-type wines — carbonated, and available in either red or white, with some of them flavored. Carbonated apple flavored wine seems to be the current favorite. And there are the pre-mixed Sangrias which bear little resemblance to the authentic Spanish Sangrias, although they are pleasant enough.

TABLE WINES

"Wine is the intellectual part of a meal, meats are merely the material part."

—Alexandre Dumas

Some Wine Talk

Americans today are more table wine-conscious than ever before—and yet, just how much do we know about these wines? And how much of what we think we know is fact? The language of wine has been developed by connoisseurs and to a large extent has remained an "inside" thing, confusing and even a little frightening to the layman.

Bouquet, aroma, young, mature, light, full-bodied, fruity, tart. We all recognize these terms, but how many of us really understand them? Perhaps it is because we don't understand them that for years we meekly accepted the suggestions of a restaurant wine steward (who, understandably, recommended his most expensive vintages) or, left on our own in the local wine shop, chose the French or German import with the most elegant label (and usually the highest price). The American wines we bought were treated like poor relations—kept for family use, *never* offered to guests. *We* liked them, but we didn't know why, and so, for special occasions, we shifted the responsibility onto a foreign label.

163

This was a silly, and usually costly, mistake.
Perhaps it's a reverse kind of snobbery, but more
and more people are discovering that they *really*
impress their guests by selecting their favorite
American wine and serving it proudly—telling
something of where it came from and how it was
made, and why they chose it to make this special
occasion even more special. Of course, they first had
to do some wine homework—and so do we all.

There are wine words that are pure snobbery and
wine words that help communicate what we like or
don't like—or simply how we feel—about a particular
wine. For wine stimulates many different reactions.
Which wine words are important? Perhaps the best
guide is the list of characteristics which professional
wine experts look for in tasting.

Here are the recommended steps for tasting wine:

1. Pour about two ounces of wine into an 8-ounce
wine glass and hold it up to the light. To check the
color and clarity, look at the wine. Is it clear, free
from sediment? Is the color true—brilliant? In reds,
the depth of color may range from the light Gamay
to the deep ruby of the Burgundy and Pinot Noir.
Color also deepens with age; a 20-year-old Pinot
Noir will seem almost black-red compared with a
younger one. In whites, the color will range from the
palest yellow Rieslings to the straw-colored
Chardonnay to the deep gold of a Sauterne.

164

2. Swirl the wine around in the glass to release its fragrance. Then sniff. Don't be afraid to really breathe it in. You'll be in good company. And you'll be amazed at the myriad scents you will catch, most of them too subtle to be caught with a polite sniff of a glass held a dainty distance away. You'll be looking for two qualities:

The first is **aroma,** the fragrance peculiar to the particular grapes from which the wine is made. For novices, it is not easy to distinguish. The best way to learn is to line up several different wines in one category. In whites, for example, take a Chardonnay, a Chenin Blanc, a Diana or Niagara, a Riesling. Sniff each one lightly. Then go to the window and take a deep breath of fresh air. Come back and sniff each one slowly and deeply, concentrating on the difference in the aroma of *fruit*. You'll soon discover that the Riesling has a light, elusive scent that disappears almost at once. (In wine jargon, this is known as a small "nose," to be compared with the "big" noses of heartier, more mature wines.) The Diana will have a pronounced grape aroma; the Chenin Blanc will be earthy, lightly tinged with sweetness.

Repeat the test with some reds. Gamay will smell strongly of the fruit. In a Cabernet, depending upon its age (when the more complex bouquet overwhelms the aroma), the grape will be less distinguishable.

The second quality you will be seeking is the **bouquet.** This is the part of the wine fragrance that comes from the fermentation and aging. The longer it has been fermented and aged, the more complex the wine. (Keep in mind that white wines are fermented and aged a much shorter period than reds, thus their bouquet is much less pronounced.) A light Riesling will have a light, almost flowery bouquet. A Niagara will be a little deeper, but still fresh and very fruity. A Chardonnay will be deeper still, richer and longer lasting.

Among the reds, the Gamay will be the lightest— though deeper than the whites. You'll find a Pinot Noir a wine of rich bouquet, but a matured Cabernet Sauvignon is *so* rich, so complex a blend of fragrances that it may even cause a bit of a tickle in your nose. Nothing quite equals the variety of delightful sensations that can be derived just from sniffing.

3. Now taste the wine. As you sip, breathe in the fragrance once more—and don't swallow immediately. Hold the wine in your mouth and swirl it around. The idea is to let the wine touch every part of your mouth, every tastebud.

Acidity, or **tartness** describes the degree of agreeable sharpness of the wine (good wine is never sour). Because of the presence of fruit acids, it is the taste which wakes you up to the wine, a reminder that this is not something to be taken for granted.

166

Astringency varies according to the amount of tannic acid in the wine, the same acid that, in tea, makes your lips pucker with pleasure. Tannin in wine comes from the seeds and skins, and, of course, the red wines are much more astringent than the whites. The Italian and Italian-type red American wines are an exception. Slightly sweeter because they are fermented a shorter time, they are less astringent, and are generally described as mellow and full-bodied. Which brings us to yet another wine word.

Body is used to describe the weight of the wine in your mouth. Water has little or no weight. Syrup has a great deal of weight. Wine, depending on the type, is thus described as light or full-bodied. A Riesling is very light. A Chardonnay is more full-bodied. Among the reds, a Pinot Noir or Burgundy will be fuller-bodied than a Cabernet or Claret.

Though the word aftertaste is not generally listed in wine glossaries, it is an important characteristic of wine — provided the aftertaste is a pleasant one! After you swallow the wine, does the flavor linger? Pleasantly? Tartly or sweetly? Does it make you crave for food, or does it stand by itself? (Many dry table wines — though intended to be consumed with a meal — stand by themselves very well. Those with a hint of sweetness go very well with just a light late-night snack, cheese and crackers or nuts.)

You will undoubtedly come across some other terms, so some brief descriptions may be helpful, although some of the following may seem elementary.

Dry   The opposite of sweet, in terms of wine. Table wines are generally dry, but some range toward sweetness. Those are properly referred to as semi-sweet.

Young   As we've seen, some wines—including most of the whites and Rosés, as well as a few reds, are meant to be drunk young, within a year or two of bottling. In these cases, the word is complimentary. But the same term applied to a Pinot Noir or Cabernet Sauvignon is a disparagement, not so much of the wine as of the person who serves it, implying that it should have been allowed to age more fully and achieve its real potential.

Harsh   A too-young wine can taste harsh, almost rough, as can a cheap, poorly made wine.

Mature   A wine that has aged fully, and is most probably in its prime.

Over-the-hill   A wine that has passed its prime and is losing, or has already lost, its freshness.

Balance   A word applied only to the finest wines, this indicates the desirable proportions of freshness and maturity, tartness and smoothness, aroma and bouquet found in top quality wines.

Table wines are the fastest growing in popularity, and they're also the least understood, perhaps because there are so many of them. Twelve to 14 percent alcohol, natural companions to food, their most familiar names are Burgundy, Bordeaux, Claret, Chablis, Rhine, and Chianti. These are the names of the great wine districts of Europe, and according to French law, only wines made within those districts may use the names. But you will find the same names on many American wines — usually the moderately priced, screw-top, half-gallon or gallon "jug" wines, which most of us drink most of the time. They are usually blended from the wines of several different grapes, and are made to resemble the European wines for which they are named.

Somewhat more expensive, because they are premium wines of finest quality, are America's varietal wines, named for the grapes which produce them. These range from the native American grapes — descendants of the same hardy vines first admired by the Vikings — with native American names like Catawba, Delaware, Niagara, Elvira, and Concord to the classic European grape varieties — Pinot Noir, Cabernet Sauvignon, Pinot Chardonnay, Riesling. Including the hybrid varieties developed to thrive in special climates in both the East and West, there are over sixty different types, sixty different wines, plus several varieties used only for blending, never by themselves.

169

As might be expected, the wines produced by the American and European grape "families" are very different. Native American grapes produce wines unlike those found anywhere else in the world, ranging from dry (Elvira) to quite sweet (Concord), while the *vinifera* grapes produce wines similar, although not exactly like, Europe's most famous types. The Pinot Noir, which produces the best French Burgundies, in California produces an outstanding wine of similar characteristics called— Pinot Noir. France's noble Bordeaux (or Clarets) are made from the Cabernet Sauvignon grape, and California Cabernet Sauvignon is justly famous for its remarkable qualities which so resemble the finest Bordeaux.

On the following charts, rather than an alphabetical listing, the wines are grouped according to type, with the most familiar generic wines heading each category.

170

RED TABLE WINES

BURGUNDY
(bur-gun-dee)

A full-flavored, full-bodied, very dry wine, blended to resemble its European namesake. Moderately priced, widely available in half-gallons and gallons, as well as in fifths.

PINOT NOIR
(pea-no no-ahr)

A rich, full-bodied varietal produced from the same grapes which go into France's best Burgundies. A premium wine that improves with age.

CHARBONO
(shar-bo-no)

A dry, full-flavored varietal produced from a grape that originated in Northern Italy.

GAMAY, GAMAY BEAUJOLAIS
(gah-may bow-jo-lay)

A dry, light-bodied varietal with a tart, fruity flavor. A fresh wine that should be drunk young.

CLARET
(klah-ret)

Dry, medium-bodied, flavorful, this blended wine is similar to the Bordeaux of France. Like American Burgundies, American Clarets come in jugs of gallons, as well as the standard fifth bottles.

CABERNET SAUVIGNON
(kab-er-nay sew-vee-nyonh)

Sometimes labeled simply "Cabernet" this noble varietal is one of America's finest premium wines, a collector's wine which improves in the bottle for as much as twenty years or more.

GRIGNOLINO
(green-yo-leen-oh)

A dry, medium-bodied varietal of Italian origin.

RUBY CABERNET

A hybrid developed principally from the Cabernet Sauvignon grape, this is a flavorful, medium-bodied wine with many of the characteristics of its parent.

CHIANTI

In America, this wine, while dry, tends to be slightly more mellow than its Italian namesake. Modestly priced, it comes in bottles of various sizes and shapes and, depending on the vintner, may bear the name "Vino Rosso."

171

OTHER RED WINES

PETITE SIRAH
(peh-tee seer-ah)

A rich, full-bodied, very dry varietal made from grapes which originated in France's Rhone Valley. Though presently produced only by a few vintners, and therefore in short supply, this wine is rapidly growing in popularity.

ZINFANDEL

Called California's "mystery" grape, because its European origin has been lost and it is now native only to California. A medium-bodied, flavorful wine, often similar to a Cabernet. It may be drunk within a year or so of bottling, but ages well and may safely be kept for several years.

WHITE TABLE WINES

CHABLIS
(sha-blee)

A dry, medium-bodied wine blended to resemble its European namesake — the white Burgundy of France. Modestly priced, this wine also comes in half-gallons and gallons, and has won high praise from wine experts who couldn't quite believe such a good wine could be so inexpensive.

PINOT CHARDONNAY
(pea-no shahr-doa-nay)

The true white Burgundy grape from which comes the great Chablis of France, this wine is full-bodied, and longer-lived than most white wines, lasting as long as three to five years.

CHENIN BLANC
(shin-in blanh)

This wine is constantly referred to as a product of "one of the lesser Burgundy grapes." It may be "lesser," but it's very *good*. Rich in aroma and bouquet, it has a distinctive earthy quality, and is full-bodied, with a pleasing aftertaste.

PINOT BLANC
(pea-no blanh)

A pleasant, if somewhat undistinguished, white Burgundy-type wine, it varies from vintner to vintner.

RHINE

This is a lighter-bodied wine, fresh in aroma, which can be almost flowery. Depending on the winemaker, Rhine wines vary in flavor from tart to almost sweet. In America, Rhine wine may be bottled in fanciful shapes and given special names by individual vintners. Most of these are priced for popular consumption.

JOHANNISBERG RIESLING
(jo-han-is-berg rees-ling)

Sometimes called Johannisberger Riesling, this grape produces the finest wines in the Rhine Valley — and in America. Light, fresh, tart, it is considered the wine best suited to lightly sauced seafood dishes.

SYLVANER
(sil-vahn-er)

Considered an inferior grape of the Rhine Valley, in California this produces a gentle white wine, softer — and thus less durable — than the true Riesling, but nonetheless pleasant.

TRAMINER
(trah-mee-ner)

Also known as Gewurztraminer (with certain varieties), this is the Alsatian grape that produces fragrant, light-bodied wines with spicy tinges to their aroma and flavors. Lovely, when at their best.

GREY RIESLING

Supposedly not a true Riesling grape at all, this variety nevertheless produces a tender wine of good flavor that will complement lightly-flavored foods which do not overwhelm its delicacy.

RIESLING

A varietal wine blended from Riesling grapes. Although with certain vintners it can be excellent, the cost differs so little from a Johannisberger that you may wish to splurge a little on that finer varietal.

EMERALD RIESLING

A California hybrid with a heritage extending back to the Johannisberger Riesling grape. Slightly sweeter than most Rhine types, with a light nose of distinct floweriness, this is growing in popularity.

173

SAUTERNE
(sew-tearn)

Sauterne (note the absence of a final "s") in America is quite different from its French counterpart. For once, the American wine tends to be much drier than its European ancestor. When labeled simply, "Sauterne," the wine is a blend, and should be priced accordingly.

SEMILLON
(say-mee-yonh)

The traditonal Sauternes (as in French Sauternes grape), this makes a medium-bodied, dry white wine with a pleasing aroma as well as flavor.

SAUVIGNON BLANC
(sew-vee-nyonh blanh)

With various vintners, this wine ranges from medium-bodied and quite dry to fuller-bodied with a hint of sweetness.

HAUT SAUTERNE
(owe sew-tearn)

Variously labeled Haut or Château, and sometimes accompanied by a registered vineyard name, this wine tends to be considerably more sweet than other American Sauterne — and closer to the European Sauternes. It is nevertheless within the province of dinner wines — though it goes better with desserts, or as an interesting contrast to salty nuts, than with the dishes that are usually accompanied by one of the drier table wines.

ROSÉ TABLE WINES

VIN ROSÉ
(van ro-zay)

Ranging from dry to slightly sweet, depending on the brand, these blended wines are popularly priced and in great demand for informal occasions — picnics, buffets, and wine-and-cheese parties.

GRENACHE ROSÉ
(grin-ash ro-zay)

A varietal made primarily from the Grenache grape, which produces the great Tavel Rosés of France, this dry, fresh wine is widely regarded as the best American Rosé and is usually the most expensive.

174

GAMAY ROSÉ (gah-may ro-zay)	A dry, fruity varietal from the same grape that produces the red Gamay. Less fragrant and slightly fuller-bodied than the Grenache Rosé, but with a pleasant flavor.
ZINFANDEL ROSÉ	Produced from the Zinfandel grape, this varietal is fuller-bodied still, and quite dry, with the distinctive flavor of the grape it comes from.

Special Wines of the Eastern United States

While American Burgundy, Claret, Chablis, and Riesling may come from either California or the East, there are a number of popular wines unique to the wine country east of the Mississippi — Ohio, Maryland, and, notably, New York. Though the grapes bear distinctly American — and most often, Indian — names, and are descendants of the vines originally found here, they are actually hybrids — the result of cross-breeding with European varieties, which has softened their naturally strong aroma and flavor.

For some reason, red wines produced in the East are poor — with the exception of a few special hybrids which are so rarely found in local shops and made by so few vintners that we will not mention them in this listing. White wine grapes have always fared better in the Eastern climes and at least one, the Catawba, produces a pleasingly soft, slightly sweet Rosé as well as a white. Here are the Eastern wines to taste:

CATAWBA (ka-tahw-bah)	Whether white or pink, this is a slightly sweet wine with a fruity aroma and taste. It is delightful with light desserts, cookies, or crackers.
CONCORD	An extremely sweet red dessert wine usually called "kosher" and often found at Jewish feasts.

175

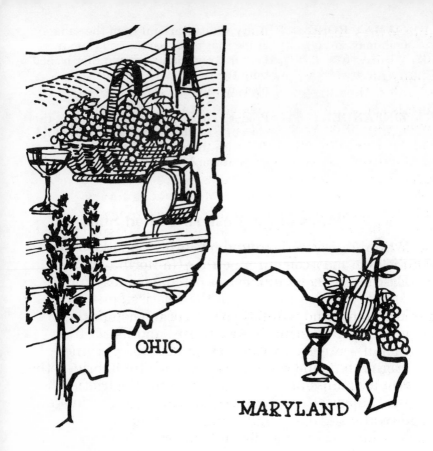

OHIO

MARYLAND

DELAWARE

A white varietal that can be either dry or semi-sweet. Depending upon the sweetness, it can go with seafood dishes or desserts.

DUTCHESS

A dry, fruity white varietal that goes equally well with fish and fowl.

NIAGARA

This semi-sweet white wine is an excellent accompaniment to desserts and light snacks.

SCUPPERNONG
(skup-er-nong)

Made from one of the hardiest Eastern varietals, this sweet white wine has the distinct fruit flavor associated with native grapes. An interesting dessert wine, and especially good with fruit and mild cheese.

176

Table Wines in the Kitchen

Reds, whites, and even Rosés are popular additions to many meat and vegetable dishes; in stews and casseroles, they are close to being indispensable. There is some question, however, as to what quality of wine should be used in cooking. That the question was ever raised at all is in some measure due to the manufacturers of "cooking" wines. As with cooking Sherry — an inferior wine with seasonings added — all "cooking wines" are invariably inferior to ordinary drinking wines. Just as invariably, the ordinary wine is a better buy, since it can be used in desserts as well as in dishes requiring the salt and herbs "cooking" wine must contain in order to remain in the nonalcoholic "beverage" class.

There are those who will tell you to "cook with the same wine you'll be drinking with the meal." But pouring half a precious bottle of Pinot Noir into the Boeuf Bourguignon is a ridiculous waste. Any American Burgundy, can be easily substituted. If wine can lose its nuances by rapid temperature changes while storing, what would you imagine happens when it simmers for an hour or so, having first been thoroughly herbed with bay leaves, thyme, a good sprinkling of monosodium glutamate, and a clove of garlic? Surely, the vintner who so lovingly turned out these bottles of vintage Pinot Noir did not envision them taking part in such a potpourri.

Common sense dictates the translation of "cook with the same wine you'll be drinking" into "cook with a wine you'd enjoy drinking," which is a wide enough latitude to include the Burgundies, Clarets, Chiantis, such whites as the Chablis and Rhine, and the Vin Rosés, as well as those drops of wine from unfinished dinner bottles you've been saving so carefully. Well-corked, these wines will remain drinkable for up to a week. After that, they'll still retain enough flavor for cooking for several more weeks.

Cooking with Red Wine

Here are some recipes, including a few classics you'll
recognize, and others that deserve to *become* classics
some of them strictly family fare, others for party
presentation. Table wine is an integral part of each
dish.

178

TABLE WINES

BEEF BOURGUIGNON

3 pounds lean beef sirloin, chuck, or round
2½ cups Burgundy
⅛ teaspoon garlic powder
⅛ teaspoon thyme
½ bay leaf
¼ cup oil
3 tablespoons flour
1 (1⅝-oz.) env. dehydrated onion soup mix
1½ cups water
5 small carrots, cut in 1-inch chunks
1 (8-oz.) can small onions
1 (4-oz.) can mushrooms or 1 dozen fresh
  mushrooms, sauteed in butter

Cut beef in 1½-inch cubes. Combine 2 cups
Burgundy, garlic powder, thyme, and bay leaf, pour
over beef and allow to stand 2 hours or longer.
Drain, saving marinade. Dry beef cubes on paper
towels. Heat oil in heavy skillet, add beef and
brown slowly on all sides. Remove beef to casserole.
Sift flour into oil remaining in skillet. Add
marinade, onion soup mix, and water. Cook and stir
until mixture boils thoroughly. Pour over beef, cover,
and bake in slow oven (300° F.) for 2 hours, or until
beef is very tender. Meanwhile, cook carrots in small
amount of boiling salted water. Drain onions and
mushrooms. Add vegetables and remaining ½ cup
Burgundy to beef. Bake 15 minutes longer, or until
vegetables are thoroughly heated. *Serves 6–8*.

COQ AU VIN

1 large frying chicken
Salt
2 tablespoons butter
2½ tablespoons cornstarch
¾ cup chicken broth
1 cup Burgundy
⅛ teaspoon thyme
Few drops bottled gravy coloring
8 small boiling onions
8 mushroom caps, fresh or canned

Season chicken with salt. Brown slowly in butter.
Remove chicken pieces to baking dish. Blend cornstarch into butter remaining in skillet. Add broth,
wine, ¾ teaspoon salt, thyme, and gravy coloring.
Cook and stir until mixture boils and is thickened.
Pour over chicken. Cover and bake in moderate oven
(350° F.) about 30 minutes, until chicken is tender.
Meanwhile, boil onions in salted water to cover until
tender; drain. Sauté fresh mushrooms in a small
amount of butter. Add onions and mushrooms to
chicken about 5 minutes before it is done. *Serves 4.*

181

DUTCH OVEN BARBEQUED LAMB

3 tablespoons bacon drippings or other fat
1 cup diced celery
$\frac{1}{2}$ cup chopped onion
2 pounds boned lamb shoulder, cubed
3 tablespoons flour
2 (8-oz.) cans tomato sauce with mushrooms
1 cup Burgundy, Claret, or other red dinner
   wine
2 tablespoons red wine vinegar
2 tablespoons brown sugar
1 teaspoon Worcestershire sauce
Salt and pepper to taste

Heat bacon drippings in a Dutch oven or other
heavy kettle; add celery and onion; sauté gently for
5 minutes. Add lamb and brown nicely on all sides.
Sprinkle flour over meat and vegetables; stir well.
Add remaining ingredients; cook, stirring constantly,
until mixture boils. Cover and simmer gently for 1
hour, or until meat is tender, stirring frequently.
Serve with rice or with baked or mashed potatoes.
Serves 5–6.

MIDDLE EAST LAMB WITH EGGPLANT

1 egg
1 cup fine soft bread crumbs
$\frac{1}{3}$ cup Burgundy or other red dinner wine
$1\frac{3}{4}$ teaspoons salt
$\frac{1}{4}$ teaspoon mixed Italian herbs
$1\frac{1}{2}$ pounds ground lean lamb
Oil
1 medium-size eggplant
Salt
Flour
$\frac{1}{2}$ cup chopped onion
1 (1-lb.) can stewed tomatoes
$\frac{1}{2}$ teaspoon mixed Italian herbs
$\frac{1}{2}$ cup Burgundy or other red dinner wine
8 ounces Mozzarella cheese, sliced
$\frac{1}{4}$ cup grated Parmesan cheese

Beat egg lightly; combine with crumbs, $\frac{1}{3}$ cup
Burgundy, $1\frac{3}{4}$ teaspoons salt, $\frac{1}{4}$ teaspoon herbs, and
ground lamb. Mix well, and shape into tiny balls.
Brown in a small amount of oil, shaking skillet to
keep balls round, and to brown them evenly. Remove
meat balls. Slice eggplant thinly. Sprinkle with salt
and dip slices in flour. Brown slowly on both sides,
adding more oil as needed. Remove from skillet.
Sauté onion lightly; add tomatoes, $\frac{1}{2}$ teaspoon herbs,
and remaining $\frac{1}{2}$ cup Burgundy. Cook uncovered
about 10 minutes, until sauce is slightly thickened.
Arrange meat balls, eggplant slices, Mozzarella, and
sauce in layers in baking dish. Sprinkle with
Parmesan cheese. Bake in moderate oven (350° F.)
20 to 25 minutes, until thoroughly heated. *Serves 6.*

GRILLED STEAK ROLL

1 top quality flank steak (about 2 pounds)
½ cup Burgundy or other red dinner wine
½ teaspoon unseasoned meat tenderizer
¼ cup finely chopped parsley
¼ cup finely chopped celery
1 green onion, finely chopped
1 teaspoon hickory smoked salt
½ teaspoon seasoned pepper

Have steak trimmed of excess fat and membrane;
score surface on both sides. Lay steak flat in a
shallow baking dish. Pour Burgundy over meat.
Marinate 1 hour or longer, turning meat several
times. Lift meat from marinade. Sprinkle one side
with meat tenderizer. Sprinkle surface with parsley,
celery, and onion. Roll up from short side like jelly
roll. Skewer or tie to hold roll together. Sprinkle
surface of meat with smoked salt and seasoned
pepper. Place meat roll on spit of rotisserie or grill.
Grill 1½ to 2 inches above heat for 50 to 60 minutes.
Brush now and then with the drained marinade. Cut
in slices to serve. Note: Two rolled flank steaks fit
nicely on a spit should one wish to serve 6 to 8
persons or cook sufficient meat for leftovers. Simply
double above recipe. Cooking time remains the same.
Serves 4.

184

CIOPPINO

1 medium-size onion
1 large clove garlic
1 sprig parsley
$\frac{1}{4}$ cup olive oil
$3\frac{1}{2}$ cups canned tomatoes
$1\frac{3}{4}$ cups canned tomato sauce
1 cup Burgundy or other red dinner wine
1 cup water
2 tablespoons wine vinegar
1 teaspoon crushed mixed Italian herbs
$1\frac{1}{2}$ teaspoons seasoned salt
$\frac{1}{2}$ teaspoon seasoned pepper
2 dozen small clams in shell
$1\frac{1}{2}$ pounds halibut or cod
1 pound prawns or large shrimp (either cooked
    or uncooked)
1 pound large crab (either cooked or uncooked)

Chop onion, garlic, and parsley fine. Cook over
moderate heat in oil until soft but not browned. Add
tomatoes, tomato sauce, wine, water, vinegar, herbs,
salt, and pepper. Bring to a boil. Reduce heat and
simmer 40 minutes. This basic sauce may be made
ahead of time, cooled and refrigerated, if desired.
Heat before adding to fish. While sauce is cooking,
rinse all fish and shellfish in cold water. Scrub clams
and allow to stand in cold salt water ($\frac{1}{4}$ cup salt to
2 quarts water) $\frac{1}{2}$ hour. Cut halibut in serving
pieces; clean prawns or shrimp; clean crab and break
into serving pieces. Layer all fish in large kettle
placing clams on top. Pour hot sauce over all. Cover
tightly and cook over low heat 20 to 25 minutes.
Serve in large heated bowls. Note: Frozen rock
lobster tails may be used in place of crab; frozen
prawns or shrimp may be substituted for fresh, and
canned clams (2 $10\frac{1}{2}$-oz., cans) will do when fresh
are not available. Or use proportionate amounts of
any fish desired.) *Serves 5–6.*

BURGUNDIE DUCK L'ORANGE

1 (4- to 5-lb.) ready-to-cook duckling
1 teaspoon salt
1 unpeeled orange
$\frac{1}{2}$ cup Burgundy or other red dinner wine
$\frac{1}{2}$ cup orange marmalade

Salt inside cavity of duck. Cut orange into eighths;
stuff into duck cavity. Fasten neck skin over back
and tie legs. Place duck, breast side up, in a shallow
pan. Pour $\frac{1}{4}$ cup Burgundy over duck. Roast in
preheated hot oven (425° F.) $\frac{1}{2}$ hour. Drain off and
discard fat. Reduce oven temperature to moderately
hot (375° F.) and continue roasting 1 hour. Heat
marmalade with remaining Burgundy; brush all of
glaze over duck and roast an additional 10 to 15
minutes. Serve with Wine Jelly (below). *Serves 4.*

Wine Jelly: Measure 2 cups wine (Sherry, Sauterne,
Burgundy, Port, Muscatel, or Rosé) into top of double
boiler. Add 3 cups sugar; mix well. Place over
rapidly boiling water and heat 3 minutes, or until
sugar is dissolved, stirring constantly. Remove from
water and at once stir in $\frac{1}{2}$ bottle fruit pectin. Pour
quickly into glasses, and immediately cover with
paraffin. Makes about 5 (6-oz.) glasses.

SPINACH BURGERS

1½ pounds ground chuck
1 (10-oz.) package frozen chopped spinach,
   thawed
½ cup Burgundy or other red dinner wine
¼ cup shredded Parmesan cheese
2 tablespoons grated onion
1½ teaspoons salt
⅛ teaspoon pepper

Combine chuck with drained spinach and all
remaining ingredients. Shape into patties. Broil, pan
fry, or barbecue meat to desired degree of doneness.
Serve with assorted relishes. *Serves 6.*

PIZZA PRONTO

1 (8-oz.) can tomato sauce with mushrooms
$1/4$ cup Burgundy or other red dinner wine
2 teaspoons cornstarch
$1/4$ teaspoon crumbled dried oregano
$1/8$ teaspoon garlic salt
$1^{1}/_{2}$ cups biscuit mix
$1/3$ cup water
1 (5-oz.) package sliced salami
1 (6-oz.) package Mozzarella cheese
$1/3$ cup grated Parmesan cheese

Blend tomato sauce, wine, cornstarch, oregano, and garlic salt together. Heat, stirring a few minutes until sauce thickens slightly. Set aside while preparing dough. Combine biscuit mix and water to make stiff dough; shape into a ball. Roll out on floured board to 10- or 12-inch circle. Fit into pizza pan; press down dough around outer edge to form a $1/2$-inch rim. Spread dough with part of tomato sauce. Top with salami (cut in pieces or rolled into small cones). Add pieces of Mozzarella cheese. Spoon on remaining sauce. Sprinkle with Parmesan and a little additional oregano, if desired. Bake in a hot oven (425° F.) about 15 minutes, or until dough is lightly browned and topping bubbly and hot. Cut into wedges to serve. *Six slices.*

MEATBALL SOUP

1 large beef soup bone
2 or 3 marrow bones
$\frac{1}{2}$ cup pearl barley
$2\frac{1}{2}$ quarts water
1 cup Burgundy or other red dinner wine
2 cups diced fresh tomatoes
1 pound ground beef chuck
$\frac{1}{2}$ cup cracker crumbs
1 egg, beaten
2 teaspoons salt
$\frac{1}{2}$ teaspoon pepper
4 medium carrots, cut into slices
3 stalks celery, with tops, sliced crosswise
1 medium onion, chopped
1 clove garlic, minced
2 small zucchini, thinly sliced
$\frac{1}{2}$ cup fresh or frozen peas

Cover bones and barley with water and wine.
Simmer, covered, 3 hours. Discard bones. Measure
broth and add water to make 2 quarts liquid. Add
tomatoes; simmer slowly while preparing meatballs.
Mix together beef chuck, cracker crumbs, egg,
1 teaspoon salt, and $\frac{1}{4}$ teaspoon pepper. Shape into
tiny meat balls about 1 inch in diameter. Drop into
simmering broth. Add carrots, celery, onion, garlic,
and remaining salt and pepper. Simmer slowly 45
minutes. Add zucchini and peas and cook 10 minutes
longer. Lace each serving with an additional
tablespoon Burgundy, if desired. *Serves 8.*

SNAPPY TONGUE

1 (4- to 5-lb.) fresh beef tongue
2 or 3 slices onion
2 or 3 stalks celery
Salt
6 peppercorns
1 bay leaf
1 cup Burgundy, Claret, or other red dinner
    wine
½ cup gingersnap crumbs
½ cup brown sugar
3 tablespoons red wine vinegar
1 lemon, thinly sliced
½ cup seedless raisins

Rinse tongue under cold running water. Place in a
kettle with the onion, celery, 1 tablespoon salt,
peppercorns, bay leaf, and wine. Add boiling water
to cover. Cover and simmer gently for about 3 hours,
or until tongue is tender. Leave tongue in stock
until cool enough to handle. Prepare sauce as
follows: Mix gingersnap crumbs and brown sugar;
stir in vinegar and 1 cup strained tongue stock.
Cook, stirring frequently, until sauce boils and
becomes smooth. Add salt to taste; stir in lemon and
raisins; simmer 2 or 3 minutes. Remove tongue from
stock and peel off skin. Place on heated platter and
serve at once with the piping hot sauce. *Serves 6.*

LIVER SAUTÉ

1 pound sliced beef liver
4 tablespoons bacon drippings or other fat
2 tablespoons minced onion
2½ tablespoons flour
1 cup consommé or bouillon-cube broth
½ cup Burgundy or other red dinner wine
1 (4-oz.) can mushroom stems and pieces,
    undrained
¾ teaspoon gravy seasoning sauce
Salt and pepper

Cut liver into small squares or strips. Heat bacon
drippings in a skillet; add onion and liver;
sauté quickly, stirring frequently, just until liver is
nicely browned; remove liver from skillet. To the
drippings add flour and blend well; stir in consommé,
wine, and mushroom stems and pieces. Cook, stirring
constantly, until sauce is thickened and smooth; add
gravy seasoning sauce and salt and pepper to
taste. Add browned liver; heat just to simmering and
serve at once on toast or with mashed potatoes or
rice. *Serves 4.*

HARVEST LOAF WITH CRANBERRY SAUCE

1½ pounds lean ground beef
1 (12-oz.) can pork luncheon meat, ground or
   minced
3 cups fine, soft bread crumbs
¾ cup milk
2 eggs, slightly beaten
2 tablespoons minced onion
Salt and pepper
1 (1-lb.) can whole cranberry sauce
½ cup brown sugar (packed)
½ cup Burgundy, Claret, or other red dinner
   wine
¼ teaspoon ground cloves
1 tablespoon cornstarch

Mix beef, luncheon meat, bread crumbs, milk, eggs, onion, salt, and pepper. Shape into loaf about 9 by 4 by 2 inches; place in a shallow baking pan. Mix cranberry sauce, sugar, wine, and cloves; stir to dissolve sugar. Spread about ¾ cup of the cranberry mixture over top of meat loaf. Bake loaf in a moderate oven (350° F.) for 1 hour, basting several times with sauce in pan. In a saucepan, blend a little of the remaining cranberry mixture with the cornstarch, stirring until smooth; add rest of cranberry mixture; stir over medium heat until mixture boils and thickens. Remove baked meat loaf from oven and let stand for 5 minutes; place on a heated platter. Slice and serve accompanied by the hot cranberry-wine sauce. *Serves 6–8.*

TREE TRIMMERS CASSEROLE

2 pounds lean beef stew meat
$\frac{1}{4}$ cup flour
2 teaspoons chili powder
2 teaspoons salt
$\frac{1}{4}$ cup shortening or oil
1 cup chopped onion
2 cloves garlic, minced
1 (1-lb.) can tomatoes
$\frac{3}{4}$ cup Burgundy or other red dinner wine
1$\frac{1}{2}$ cups rice
1 (12-oz.) can whole kernel corn
1 tablespoon butter

Cut beef in small cubes, and dredge with flour, chili powder, and salt. Brown in shortening. Add onion, and brown lightly, stirring frequently. Stir in any of remaining flour mixture. Add garlic, tomatoes, and Burgundy; cover and simmer 1$\frac{1}{2}$ to 2 hours, or until meat is tender. Meanwhile, steam or boil rice. Drain corn, if necessary, and heat with butter. Turn beef mixture into serving dish, and spoon corn into a circle on top. Mound rice in center. *Serves 6.*

PRIME RIBS CHATEAU*

7–8 ribs roast of beef
Whole cloves
Sliced onion
Salt and pepper
1 cup Burgundy wine

Have your butcher separate the bones from the meat, along with the "cap"—the layer of fat atop the meat. Then have him re-tie the roast, with bones and "cap." The day before serving, untie the roast, remove "cap," salt and pepper, and place a layer of sliced onions and a generous sprinkling of whole cloves, replace "cap" and re-tie roast. Let stand overnight.

The day of serving, place in 325° oven for 2½ hours— it will be rare in the center, slightly well done at the outer edges.

Pour over the entire roast a cup of Burgundy wine and let it steep at least an hour. The wine will mingle with the meat juices to produce an extraordinary sauce.

To serve, reheat in a warm oven, discard the cap and bones, and slice to desired thickness for each guest. *Serves 8 to 10.*

*The Chateau is a charming 19th-century inn in Stamford, New York. This is owner Jim Winig's own recipe for Prime Ribs—the star of The Chateau's gourmet menu.

ITALIAN POT ROAST

1 (3-pound) beef chuck roast
1 tablespoon salt
½ teaspoon pepper
1 (No. 2-½) can tomatoes
1 teaspoon mixed Italian herbs
¼ cup instant minced onion or 1 cup finely
  chopped raw onion
1 cup Burgundy or other red dinner wine
¼ teaspoon garlic powder or 2 finely chopped
  cloves garlic
2 tablespoons cornstarch
Hot cooked brown rice or noodles

Sprinkle roast with salt and pepper; brown slowly in hot skillet rubbed with fat trimmed from meat. Add all remaining ingredients except cornstarch and rice. Cover and simmer until meat is tender — about 2 hours. Transfer meat to cutting board and slice, cutting across the grain. Thicken gravy with cornstarch mixed with a little cold water, if desired. Serve meat and gravy over brown rice or noodles. *Makes 4 servings.*

LIVER AND BACON BURGUNDY EN BROCHETTE

1 pound sliced beef liver
6 slices bacon
1 cup Burgundy or other red dinner wine
Onion salt and pepper
3 slices toast
Parsley

Cut liver into small pieces (36 is the ideal number);
cut each strip of bacon into 6 pieces. Alternate pieces
of liver and bacon on 6 wooden or metal skewers.
Lay filled skewers in a shallow pan; pour wine over
them; let stand 1 hour or longer, turning the
skewers occasionally. Remove skewers from wine
and suspend between the sides of a loaf pan; sprinkle
with onion salt and pepper. Bake in a hot oven
(350° F.) for 15 to 20 minutes, basting several times
with the wine. To serve, lay 2 skewers on each piece
of toast, and pour some of the pan drippings over
all. Garnish with parsley. *Serves 3.*

SAUERBRATEN

4 to 5 pounds beef chuck, rolled and tied
1 cup Burgundy or Claret
½ cup red wine vinegar
½ cup water
2 onions, sliced
3 bay leaves
10 whole peppercorns
10 whole cloves
1 tablespoon sugar
1 teaspoon dry mustard
¼ teaspoon each thyme and powdered ginger
1 teaspoon salt
3 tablespoons bacon drippings or other fat

Place meat in a large bowl. Combine all remaining ingredients except fat; pour over meat. Cover and let stand in the refrigerator for 3 or 4 days, turning meat each day. Remove meat from marinade. Dry meat thoroughly with paper towels. Strain marinade. Heat bacon drippings in a Dutch oven or other large, heavy kettle; brown meat slowly on all sides. Pour strained marinade over meat. Cover and simmer very gently for about 3 hours, or until meat is tender, turning meat occasionally. *Serves 8 to 10.*

BAKED BEEFSTEAK ROLLS WITH VEGETABLES

2 lbs. round steak, cut ¼ inch thick
Salt and pepper
½ pound bulk sausage meat
½ cup chopped onion
½ cup chopped celery
¼ cup chopped green pepper
Flour
¼ cup bacon drippings or other fat
¾ cup boiling water
¾ cup Burgundy or Claret
4 medium-sized carrots, cut crosswise in halves
and lengthwise in quarters
4 medium-sized zucchini, cut lengthwise in
quarters

Cut round steak in pieces about 4 by 2 inches; sprinkle with salt and pepper. Using a wooden mallet, a hammer or the edge of a heavy plate, pound pieces to flatten them slightly. Cook sausage meat, onion, celery and green pepper together very gently for 10 minutes, stirring with a fork so that sausage meat is broken into small bits. Sprinkle ¼ cup flour over sausage meat and vegetables; mix well. Spread pieces of steak with this mixture; roll up jelly-roll fashion, from one short side to the other; fasten with skewers or string. Dredge rolls with flour; brown on all sides in the bacon drippings. Place rolls in a roasting pan; add water and wine; season with salt and pepper. Cover and bake in a moderate oven (350° F.) for ½ hour. Arrange carrots and zucchini around rolls; continue baking for 1¼ to 1½ hours, or until meat and vegetables are tender. Baste occasionally, and add a little more water or wine if gravy cooks down too much. Remove skewers or string from rolls; place on heated platter and surround with vegetables; pour gravy over all. Good with mashed or baked potatoes, noodles or rice. *Serves 6.*

PARMESAN POLENTA CASSEROLE

In top of a double boiler mix 1½ cups polenta or yellow cornmeal with 1½ cups cold water; add 3 cups boiling water and 1½ teaspoons salt. Stir over direct heat until mixture boils and thickens, then place over boiling water, cover and cook 1 hour. Add 1 cup diced Mozzarella cheese and 3 tablespoons butter or margarine, and stir until blended. Spoon mixture in the shape of a ring on a heated platter. Pour Beef Sauce in center and over ring. Sprinkle with additional grated Parmesan cheese. Serve at once.

Beef Sauce:

1 lb. ground beef
1 large onion, chopped
1 clove garlic, chopped
2 tablespoons salad oil
2 cups canned tomatoes
1 (8 oz.) can tomato sauce
¼ cup canned tomato paste
½ cup Burgundy or other red table wine
1 teaspoon sugar
¼ teaspoon each: sweet basil, rosemary and
    oregano
Salt and pepper to taste

In electric skillet sauté meat, onion and garlic in oil until meat is no longer red, stirring with a fork so that meat is broken into small bits. Add remaining ingredients. Cover and simmer 1½ hours, stirring occasionally. (Sauce may be prepared ahead of time and reheated before serving.) *Serves 6.*

MULLED WINE DIP

1 cup Burgundy, Zinfandel or other red dinner
  wine
$\frac{1}{4}$ cup brown sugar (packed)
2 teaspoons cornstarch
$\frac{1}{8}$ teaspoon each cinnamon and allspice
Dash cloves

Turn wine into fondue pot and heat. Meanwhile,
blend sugar, cornstarch and spices together. Stir
into hot wine, and cook until clear and slightly
thickened, stirring frequently. Turn heat low to keep
warm for serving. Use as dip for wedges of fresh
fruit such as apple, winter pear, pineapple chunks
or strawberries. Firm cake or lady fingers may be
dipped in this sauce also. (Note: To make in an
electric fondue pot, turn heat control to medium
to heat wine. Stir in the sugar-spice mixture and
cook until thickened, then turn to low heat to keep
warm.) *Makes 1 cup.*

CHERRY CRUNCH SUNDAE SAUCE

1½ tablespoons cornstarch
¾ cup sugar
Dash of salt
½ cup Burgundy or other red table wine
½ cup orange juice
1 tablespoon lemon juice
1 teaspoon grated lemon rind
Dash of mace
Red food coloring, if desired
1 cup halved, pitted fresh or canned dark, sweet
   red cherries
½ cup coarsely chopped walnuts
2 tablespoons butter or margarine

Mix cornstarch, sugar and salt in a saucepan;
gradually stir in wine, orange juice and lemon juice,
blending until mixture is smooth. Cook and stir over
medium heat until mixture boils, thickens and
becomes clear. Add lemon rind, mace and a few
drops of red coloring, if desired. Add cherries and
nuts; simmer 5 minutes. Add butter. Serve warm or
cold over vanilla ice cream. *Makes 2 cups.*

BURGUNDY APPLE SAUCE

1 ½ tablespoons cornstarch
1 cup sugar
Dash of salt
½ teaspoon cinnamon
½ teaspoon nutmeg
¾ cup Burgundy or other red dinner wine
¾ cup bottled apple juice
1 ½ tablespoons lemon juice
1 ½ teaspoons grated lemon peel
2 tablespoons butter or margarine

Mix cornstarch, sugar, salt and spices in a saucepan;
gradually stir in wine and apple juice, mixing until
perfectly smooth. Stir over medium heat until
mixture boils and thickens; continue cooking a
minute or two, until clear. Remove from heat; add
lemon juice, lemon peel and butter. Serve hot over
warm apple pie, apple turnovers, apple crisp, apple
dumplings or other warm apple dessert. Or use as a
sauce for steamed pudding. *Makes about 2 cups.*

CLARET PITCHER PUNCH

1 (6-oz.) can frozen orange juice
2 cups Claret, Burgundy or other red dinner
   wine
1½ tablespoons powdered sugar (or to taste)
Ice cubes

Mix orange juice and wine in a pitcher; add sugar
and stir until dissolved. Add a generous amount
of ice cubes and stir until thoroughly chilled. Pour
into punch cups or small glasses. (Note: If preferred,
the sweetened orange juice-Claret mixture may be
poured over a block of ice in a punch bowl instead
of being served from a pitcher.)

JELLIED APPLE BLUSH PIE

1 envelope unflavored gelatin
$\frac{1}{4}$ cup cold water
$\frac{2}{3}$ cup bottled apple juice
$\frac{1}{3}$ cup Burgundy or other red dinner wine
1 cup sugar
$\frac{1}{2}$ teaspoon cinnamon
$\frac{1}{4}$ teaspoon nutmeg
1 teaspoon grated lemon peel
1 teaspoon lemon juice
1 tablespoon butter or margarine
Red food coloring
1 (No. 2) can sliced pie apples, drained
1 (9-inch) baked pastry shell
Whipped cream

Soften gelatin in the cold water 5 minutes. Combine apple juice, wine, sugar, cinnamon, nutmeg and lemon peel in a saucepan; bring to a boil, stirring until sugar is dissolved; simmer 5 minutes. Remove from heat; add lemon juice, butter and softened gelatin; stir until gelatin is dissolved. Add enough red food coloring to give mixture a nice rosy hue. Cool, then chill until syrupy, stirring occasionally. Arrange half of the apple slices in bottom of pie shell; cover with half of the partially thickened gelatin mixture. Repeat with remaining apple slices and gelatin mixture. Chill until firm. Before serving, garnish top of pie with whipped cream.

CRANBERRY SPARKLE

2 ($\frac{4}{5}$-qt.) bottles Burgundy or other red wine
1 pint cranberry juice cocktail
2 (12-oz.) cans lemon-lime carbonated beverage

Refrigerate all ingredients for several hours. Just before serving, combine them in a large pitcher or punch bowl. Serve in wine glasses or over ice cubes in tall glasses. (Note: The two "fifth" bottles of wine may be replaced by one half gallon, if desired. This changes the proportion of wine to other ingredients slightly, but not enough to influence flavor.)
Makes 18 five-oz. servings.

PINK LEMONADE PIE

1 envelope unflavored gelatin
$1/3$ cup Burgundy or other red wine
4 eggs, separated
$1\frac{1}{4}$ cups sugar
Dash of salt
1 teaspoon grated lemon rind
$1/2$ cup lemon juice
1 cup heavy cream
Red food coloring
1 (9-inch) baked pie shell

Soften gelatin in the wine. Beat egg yolks slightly
in top of a double boiler; stir in 1 cup sugar, salt,
lemon rind and lemon juice; cook, stirring, over
boiling water until mixture thickens. Add softened
gelatin; stir until dissolved. Cool until mixture
begins to thicken. Beat egg whites stiff with
remaining $1/4$ cup sugar; whip $1/2$ cup of the cream;
fold egg whites and cream into lemon mixture.
Gently stir in a few drops of red food coloring, just
enough to give a pleasantly pink effect. Pour into
pie shell; chill until firm. Before serving, whip
remaining $1/2$ cup cream and spread over top of pie.

BEEF AND VEGETABLE PIE BURGUNDY

2 tablespoons bacon drippings or other fat
2 pounds beef stew meat, cubed
1 large onion, thinly sliced
3 cups boiling water
1 cup Burgundy or Claret
2 or 3 sprigs parsley
1 bay leaf
2 whole cloves
1 teaspoon monosodium glutamate
Salt and pepper to taste
2 cups diced raw potatoes
1 cup diced raw carrots
Flour
Pastry for top of pie

Heat bacon drippings in a Dutch oven or other heavy
kettle; add meat and onion; cook, stirring frequently,
until meat is nicely browned. Add water, wine,
parsley, bay leaf, cloves, monosodium glutamate,
salt and pepper. Cover and simmer gently, stirring
occasionally, for 1½ hours. Add potatoes and carrots;
continue cooking for ½ hour, or until meat and
vegetables are tender. Transfer meat and vegetables
to a greased 2-quart casserole.

Make gravy as follows: Strain and measure liquid;
return liquid to Dutch oven. Allow 2 tablespoons
flour per cup of liquid; blend with a little cold water
to make a thin paste. Pour this mixture slowly into
liquid in Dutch oven, stirring constantly to prevent
lumping. Cook, stirring constantly, until gravy boils
and thickens. Taste and add more salt and pepper
if necessary.

Pour gravy over meat and vegetables. Cover with
pastry rolled ⅛ inch thick; cut gashes in top to
permit escape of steam. Bake in hot oven (450° F.)
for 15 minutes. *Serves 6.*

BEEF AND PORK GOULASH

2 tablespoons bacon drippings or other fat
1 pound beef stew meat, cubed
1 pound lean pork, cubed
1 large onion, minced
¼ teaspoon paprika
3 tablespoons flour
¾ cup water
½ cup Burgundy, Claret or other red wine
1 (4-oz.) can mushroom stems and pieces,
   undrained
Salt and pepper
1 cup dairy sour cream

Heat bacon drippings in a large, heavy skillet or a
Dutch oven. Add beef, pork and onion; sprinkle with
paprika; sauté, stirring frequently, until meat is
nicely browned. Sprinkle flour over meat and stir
well; add water, wine, mushrooms (including liquid),
salt and pepper; cook, stirring constantly, until
gravy boils and thickens. Cover and simmer gently,
stirring frequently, for about 2 hours, or until meat
is very tender. Just before serving, stir in sour
cream; taste and add additional salt and pepper, if
necessary. Serve with noodles, rice or mashed
potatoes. *Makes 5 or 6 servings.*

BEEF AS IN BURGUNDY

4 pounds beef bottom round
$\frac{1}{3}$ cup flour
2 teaspoons salt
$\frac{1}{4}$ teaspoon pepper
4 thin slices salt pork
3 tablespoons brandy
2 medium-sized onions
3 carrots
2 tablespoons butter or margarine
3 sprigs parsley
2 bay leaves
$\frac{1}{4}$ teaspoon thyme
1 crushed clove garlic
3 cups Burgundy or other red wine
1 cup sliced fresh mushrooms (or 1 4-oz. can)
1 tablespoon tomato paste

Cut meat into 1½-inch cubes. Combine flour, salt
and pepper in a paper bag and shake beef cubes, a
few at a time, to coat well with flour. Fry salt pork
in Dutch oven or large skillet; push to one side, add
beef and brown on all sides. Pour the brandy over
the meat and set it aflame. Peel and slice onions and
carrots; melt butter in a separate pan; add the
vegetables and cook until soft and yellow, about
5 minutes. Add to the meat along with parsley, bay
leaves, thyme and garlic. Stir in wine, enough water
to cover the meat — about 2 cups — and cover pan
tightly. Simmer until meat is almost tender, about
2½ hours. Add mushrooms and tomato paste, and
simmer 30 minutes longer. *Makes 8 to 10 servings.*

BARBECUED CHUCK STEAK

¼ cup Burgundy or other red wine
¼ cup oil
1 tablespoon wine vinegar
½ teaspoon unseasoned meat tenderizer
½ teaspoon onion powder
½ teaspoon mixed Italian herbs
½ teaspoon seasoned salt
1 onion, sliced
2 or 3 small parsley sprigs
2 to 2½ lb. chuck steak

Combine all ingredients except meat. Place chuck steak in shallow pan, prick with a fork, and pour marinade over it. Cover and refrigerate overnight, turning steak once or twice. Drain well. Grill or broil 3 to 4 minutes on each side, until meat is well browned and rare inside, brushing often with marinade. *Serves 4 or 5.*

BEEF TACOS

1 pound ground beef
1 tablespoon oil
1 teaspoon salt
2 (8-oz.) cans tomato sauce
1 cup Burgundy or other red wine
$\frac{1}{8}$ teaspoon garlic powder
2 teaspoons chili powder
1 tablespoon instant minced onion
Fresh, frozen or canned tortillas
Butter or margarine
Shredded lettuce
Grated American cheese

Brown beef in hot oil; add salt, tomato sauce, wine,
garlic and chili powders and instant minced onion.
Simmer, stirring occasionally, until sauce is thick —
15 to 20 minutes. Toast tortillas one at a time,
placing them on a wire rack over a hot flame or
electric burner.* Heat them until they soften — about
30 seconds on each side. Immediately spread with
butter, spoon meat filling on half of tortilla and top
with shredded lettuce and cheese. Fold over other
half of tortilla and secure with toothpick. Serve
immediately. *Makes about 8 servings.*

*May be done on grill outdoors. Toast tortillas directly on grill high above
heat. Keep filling hot on edge of grill.

HOLIDAY SPICED WINE

1 quart water
3 cups sugar
12 whole cloves
4 inches stick cinnamon
6 whole allspice
$1/2$ teaspoon powdered ginger
Rind of 1 orange
Rind of 1 lemon
2 cups orange juice
1 cup lemon juice
1 ($4/5$ qt.) bottle Burgundy or Claret

Combine water, sugar, spices, orange rind and lemon rind in a saucepan. Bring to a boil, stirring until sugar is dissolved; simmer 10 minutes. Remove from heat and let stand 1 hour. Strain. Add orange juice, lemon juice and wine; heat gently. *Do not boil.* Serve hot in pottery mugs or coffee mugs. *Makes about $2^1/2$ quarts.*

212

CHEESE BURGUNDIES

4 cups shredded American Cheddar cheese
¾ cup Burgundy, Claret or other red dinner
wine
2 tablespoons chopped onion (optional)
4 hamburger buns cut in half

Marinate cheese in wine and allow to stand for one
hour. Add onion if desired, mix thoroughly and spoon
on halved hamburger buns. Broil until cheese melts.
Serve at once.

Cooking with White Wine

PATÉ IN PASTRY

$^2/_3$ cup minced onion
3 tablespoons butter
$^2/_3$ cup Sauterne or other white dinner wine
1 pound ground veal
1 pound ground pork shoulder (including some fat)
3 eggs, beaten lightly
$2^1/_2$ teaspoons salt
$^1/_4$ teaspoon pepper
$^1/_4$ teaspoon thyme
Dash of cayenne
3 sticks pastry mix

Sauté onion in butter until transparent but not browned. Add Sauterne and simmer until liquid is reduced to about $^1/_3$ cup. Cool slightly. Combine meats, eggs, salt, pepper, thyme, and cayenne. Add onion-wine mixture and beat with a fork until light and fluffy. Turn into loaf pan about $8^1/_2$ by $4^1/_2$ by $2^1/_2$ inches, packing with a fork to avoid any air pockets. Bake in moderate oven (350° F.) 1 hour 15 minutes, covering pan loosely with foil after 30 minutes, so a heavy crust is not formed on top. Cool meat in pan, then turn out and scrape off any jellied juices.

Prepare pastry mix as package directs. Roll out about $^3/_4$ of the pastry into a sheet about $8^1/_2$ by $12^1/_2$ inches. Invert baked paté loaf, and fit pastry over bottom, sides and ends. Divide remaining pastry in half, and roll each piece to a thin sheet large enough to cover top of loaf. Invert loaf onto baking sheet and cover top with one of the sheets, moistening and overlapping edges, and pressing them firmly together. Cover top of loaf with second sheet, arranging it to cover lapped edges completely. Cut a $^1/_2$-inch hole in center to allow steam to escape. With pastry trimmings, make small cutouts in any desired shape and arrange in pattern over top. Brush with lightly beaten egg white. Bake in hot oven (425° F.) for about 45 minutes, until pastry is nicely browned. Cool before cutting.

216

OYSTER TARTS FLORENTINE

1 (8-oz.) can oysters
²/₃ cup oyster liquor and cream
2 tablespoons finely chopped onion
1½ tablespoons butter
¼ cup sifted flour
²/₃ cup Sauterne
Salt and pepper
1 cup finely chopped, well-drained, cooked
  spinach
2⅓ to 3 dozen small tart shells (2 by 1¾ inches),
  baked

Drain oyster liquor into measuring cup; add cream to
reach the ²/₃ cup level. Chop oysters. Cook onion in
butter until soft but not browned. Stir in flour.
Slowly stir in oyster-cream mixture, then wine. Cook
and stir until sauce boils and thickens. Add salt
and pepper to taste. Stir in well-drained spinach
and chopped oysters. Spoon into tart shells. Bake in
a moderately hot oven (375° F.) until heated, 10 to
15 minutes. Serve warm. *Makes about 3 dozen tarts.*

CHILLED SUMMER SOUP

1 medium-size cucumber
2 green onions
½ small green pepper
1 sprig parsley
1 tablespoon prepared horseradish
1 tablespoon sugar
1 teaspoon salt
1 (7-oz.) can minced clams
3 cups buttermilk
1 cup Chablis

Pare cucumber; trim onions; seed green pepper. Cut vegetables in medium-size pieces and turn into blender container along with parsley, horseradish, sugar, salt, undrained clams, and 2 cups buttermilk. Cover and blend at high speed until mixture is smooth. Pour into storage container; add remaining buttermilk and wine. Stir well to blend. Cover and chill several hours or overnight. *Serves 6.*

SCAMPI

4 tablespoons butter or margarine
$\frac{1}{8}$ teaspoon minced garlic
2 tablespoons parsley flakes
$\frac{1}{2}$ cup Chablis
2 (4$\frac{1}{2}$-oz.) cans large shrimp, well drained

Melt butter or margarine over medium heat in a
small skillet or chafing dish. Add garlic, parsley,
and wine. Heat to simmering, add shrimp, and cook
over low heat until hot through, about 5 minutes.
Serve very hot with toast squares. *Serves 2.*

SALMON WITH SOUR CREAM SAUCE

¼ cup Sauterne
1 cup dairy sour cream
¼ cup mayonnaise
⅛ teaspoon curry powder
1 tablespoon instant minced onion
1 canned green chili, chopped, or 2 tablespoons
  chopped green pepper
½ teaspoon salt
Baked, broiled, or fried salmon

Stir wine into sour cream. Add all remaining
ingredients, except salmon, and blend well.
Refrigerate for several hours to blend flavors. Serve
over baked, broiled, or fried salmon. *Serves 6.*

220

PINEAPPLE CHICKEN SAUTÉ

1 (9-oz.) can pineapple tidbits
1 (3½-lb.) frying chicken cut in serving pieces
Salt and pepper
2 tablespoons butter or margarine
2 tablespoons salad oil
2 tablespoons flour
½ cup Sauterne
¼ cup water
2 tablespoons wine vinegar
1 tablespoon brown sugar
1 tablespoon soy sauce
1 green pepper, cut in thin strips

Drain pineapple, reserving syrup. Dust chicken
with salt and pepper. Heat butter and oil in a large,
heavy skillet; brown chicken nicely on all sides.
Remove chicken from skillet. Add flour to drippings
and blend well; add reserved pineapple syrup, wine,
water, and vinegar; cook, stirring constantly, until
mixture boils and thickens. Add brown sugar and
soy sauce. Return chicken to skillet. Cover and
simmer gently for 40 to 50 minutes, or until
chicken is almost tender, turning and basting
occasionally. Add drained pineapple and green
pepper; cover and continue cooking 10 minutes.
Serves 4.

CHICKEN MARENGO

2 medium onions, chopped
$^{1}/_{4}$ cup oil
1 clove garlic, finely chopped
1 teaspoon basil
$^{3}/_{4}$ teaspoon thyme
1 (1-lb. 12-oz.) can tomatoes
$^{3}/_{4}$ cup Rhine or other white dinner wine
1 (4-oz.) can mushrooms, undrained
2 (3-inch) strips orange peel
1 teaspoon salt
$^{1}/_{2}$ small bay leaf
2 cups cooked chicken (or 1 (12$^{1}/_{2}$-oz.) can tuna
    or 2 (5-oz.) cans shrimp)

Cook onion in oil until transparent and lightly browned. Add garlic, basil, thyme, and cook 2 or 3 minutes longer, stirring frequently. Add tomatoes, wine, mushrooms, orange peel, salt, and bay leaf, and simmer about 1 hour. Remove orange peel and bay leaf. Add chicken or drained, coarsely flaked tuna and heat. Serve in hot Polenta Ring. (Following.) *Serves 6–8.*

SPICY FRUITED CHICKEN

1 (5-lb.) roasting chicken
Salt and pepper
1 onion, peeled and halved
2 stalks celery, halved
$\frac{1}{4}$ cup melted shortening (half butter)
$\frac{3}{4}$ cup syrup from spiced fruit (such as, pears,
   peaches, figs, watermelon preserves)
$\frac{1}{4}$ cup wine vinegar
1 cup Chablis
$\frac{3}{4}$ teaspoon powdered rosemary or ginger
Assorted spiced fruits

Season inside of chicken with salt and pepper. Insert
onion and celery in cavity; truss chicken for roasting.
Place in pan; brush on the melted shortening and
sprinkle outside with salt and pepper. Place in a
very hot oven (450° F.) for 10 to 15 minutes, just
until chicken begins to take on color. Reduce heat to
moderate (350° F.) and roast, uncovered, $\frac{1}{2}$ hour.
Shake remaining ingredients, except fruits, in a
covered jar until well blended. Spoon about $\frac{1}{4}$ of the
mixture over chicken. Continue to roast, basting
often with remaining mixture, until chicken is
tender, about 1 hour longer. A square of foil may be
placed loosely over chicken the last half hour of
cooking if a light brown skin color is desired. Serve
with the rich pan juices (fat removed) as a thin
gravy. Or, for thicker gravy, skim off all but 2
tablespoons of the fat. Thicken juices slightly with
a little cornstarch blended with cold water. Arrange
chicken on serving platter and garnish lavishly with
an assortment of spiced fruits. *Serves 4.*

POLENTA RING

3 cups chicken broth
1 cup Sauterne or other white dinner wine
1½ cups corn meal
4 teaspoons salt
2 eggs, beaten
¾ cup grated Parmesan cheese

Combine 1½ cups chicken broth with wine in top of
double boiler, and bring to boil over direct heat. Stir
corn meal into remaining 1½ cups broth; then stir
slowly into hot broth. Add salt and cook 2 or 3
minutes, stirring constantly, until very thick. Place
over boiling water, cover and cook 15 to 20 minutes
longer. Slowly stir into beaten eggs and cheese.
Spoon into oiled 8½-inch ring mold. Bake in
moderate oven (350° F.) for 5 minutes. Unmold
carefully onto serving plate and fill with hot
Chicken Marengo.

WINE-BASTED GAME HENS

2 (14- to 16-oz. size) Rock Cornish hens
Celery
Onion
Seasoned salt
Pepper
⅓ cup butter
½ cup Sauterne
⅓ cup orange juice
1 tablespoon lemon juice

Remove giblets from Cornish hens. If desired, cook
them in lightly salted water to cover with a stalk of
celery and ½ a small onion until tender in small
covered pan. Use this broth and finely chopped
cooked giblets in making pan sauce to serve with
the roasted hens. Sprinkle inside cavity of each bird
with seasoned salt and pepper; place small piece
celery and onion inside each. Truss birds using
wooden picks and tying legs together with string.
Place birds in small shallow pan. Pour melted butter
over birds. Sprinkle with seasoned salt and pepper.
Roast in a very hot oven (450° F.) 20 minutes. Spoon
on wine, orange and lemon juices. Continue roasting,
basting often with pan sauce, until birds are tender
and nicely browned, about 40 minutes longer.
Remove birds to hot plate and keep warm. If making
pan sauce, skim off any excess fat from juices in
pan. Stir ½ cup giblet broth into pan. Bring to boil
loosening all brown particles. Taste and correct
seasoning, if needed. Add chopped giblets. Spoon a
little of the rich pan sauce over each hen when
served. *Serves 2.*

BEEF STROGANOFF

3 pounds sirloin of beef
$\frac{1}{2}$ cup shortening (half butter or margarine)
$1\frac{1}{4}$ cups Chablis
1 ($10\frac{1}{2}$-oz.) can beef bouillon
1 teaspoon seasoned or garlic salt
1 teaspoon seasoned pepper
$\frac{1}{4}$ teaspoon dried dill
3 tablespoons flour
$\frac{1}{2}$ pound fresh mushrooms, halved or sliced
$\frac{1}{2}$ cup chopped green or mild onion
$1\frac{1}{2}$ cups dairy sour cream
Small whole tomatoes or wedges, lemon slices,
   and parsley for garnish

Trim any fat from beef; cut into small cubes not
over 1 inch in diameter. Brown beef quickly in heavy
skillet in some of the shortening to a rich, deep
color. Brown about $\frac{1}{4}$ of the meat at a time,
removing meat as it browns; then continue with
another portion until entire amount is done. Drain
off any remaining fat, leaving rich brown drippings
in pan. Stir 1 cup wine and bouillon into drippings.
Sprinkle in salt, pepper, and dill; add browned meat,
cover tightly, and simmer until tender, about 40
minutes. Blend flour to smooth paste with remaining
$\frac{1}{4}$ cup wine. Stir into meat in pan. Cook until sauce
thickens, about 10 minutes. Cook mushrooms and
onion in fat drained from browning meat (or in an
additional 3 or 4 tablespoons) just until tender-crisp.
Drain and add to beef. Stir in sour cream and turn
into chafing dish to keep hot. Garnish with tomatoes,
lemon slices, and sprigs of parsley. *Serves 8.*

KOREAN SHORTRIBS

4 pounds beef shortribs
½ cup soy sauce
½ cup Sauterne or other white dinner wine
¼ cup sliced green onions
2 tablespoons sesame seeds
2 tablespoons sugar
2 cloves garlic, minced or crushed
½ teaspoon pepper
¼ teaspoon monosodium glutamate

Trim shortribs and cut into 2½-inch cubes. Score ribs
(with bone side down), cutting part way through
about ½ inch apart. Combine all remaining
ingredients. Pour over meat and marinate 4 to 5
hours. Grill over hot coals, bone side down. When
brown, turn and cook on meat side. Lift and turn
meat throughout cooking time (about 15 minutes)
to expose all surfaces to heat. Cook until crisply
brown. *Serves 4.*

HERBED BAKED PORK CHOPS

4 pork chops, cut 1 inch thick
Flour
Salt and pepper
1 medium-size onion, very thinly sliced
Pinch each of thyme and rosemary
$\frac{1}{2}$ cup Sauterne
$1\frac{1}{2}$ cups water

Dredge pork chops with flour seasoned with salt and pepper. Brown well on both sides in heavy skillet or a Dutch oven, using a little fat trimmed from the chops or bacon drippings. Cover with onion slices; sprinkle with thyme and rosemary. Pour wine and $\frac{1}{2}$ cup of the water over all. Cover and bake in a slow oven (325° F.) for 2 hours, basting occasionally. Remove chops to a heated platter. Mix 1 tablespoon flour and remaining 1 cup water until smooth; add to juices in skillet; cook, stirring constantly, until mixture boils and thickens. Season gravy to taste with salt and pepper; pour over chops. *Serves 4.*

BARBECUE BEEFBURGER LOAF

1½ pounds ground lean beef
½ cup Sauterne
1 tablespoon instant minced onion
1 teaspoon salt
½ cup soft stale bread crumbs
1 long or round loaf French bread
Butter or margarine
Thinly sliced tomatoes
Thinly sliced avocados
Seasoned salt

Mix beef, wine, onion, salt, and bread crumbs lightly
but thoroughly. Pat to about ½ inch larger than loaf
of bread. Grill meat to desired degree of doneness.
Meanwhile, split loaf of bread in half horizontally.
Toast over grill. Spread cut sides of bread with
butter and place bottom half of loaf on hot serving
platter. Top with grilled meat; arrange tomato and
avocado slices over top; sprinkle with seasoned salt.
Cover with top of loaf. Cut in diagonal slices to
serve. *Serves 6–8.*

SWEET 'N SOUR HAM ROLLS

1 pound ground chuck
$\frac{1}{4}$ cup milk
$\frac{1}{2}$ cup Sauterne, Chablis, or other white dinner
  wine
$\frac{1}{4}$ cup dry bread crumbs
$\frac{1}{3}$ cup finely chopped onion
$\frac{1}{2}$ teaspoon salt
Dash of pepper
6 thin slices boiled ham (6$\frac{1}{2}$ by 4 inches)
2 tablespoons butter or margarine
$\frac{1}{2}$ cup brown sugar (packed)
2 tablespoons cornstarch
2 teaspoons prepared mustard
1 (13$\frac{1}{2}$-oz.) can grapefruit sections

Mix ground chuck lightly with milk, $\frac{1}{4}$ cup of the
wine, crumbs, onion, salt, and pepper. Spoon $\frac{1}{6}$ of
mixture onto each ham slice. Roll ham around meat.
Arrange with seam side down in shallow baking pan
(about 9 by 12 inches). Melt butter; blend in brown
sugar, cornstarch, mustard, remaining $\frac{1}{4}$ cup wine,
and grapefruit juice from can; bring to boil; and
pour over meat rolls. Bake in moderate oven
(350° F.) about 30 minutes, basting occasionally.
Stir grapefruit into sauce around meat and bake
15 minutes longer. *Serves 6.*

HAM LOAF IN PASTRY

Ham Loaf

2 eggs
½ cup Sauterne
1 cup soft bread crumbs
1 teaspoon salt
1 teaspoon dry mustard
¼ teaspoon white pepper
¾ pound ground lean pork
¾ pound ground veal
1½ pounds ground raw ham
½ cup sliced pimiento-stuffed green olives

Beat eggs lightly. Add wine, bread crumbs, salt, mustard, and pepper; mix well. Add meats, and beat with a fork until well blended. Mix in olives. Pack into oiled loaf pan (about 10 by 5 by 2½ inches). Bake in moderate oven (350° F.) 1¼ hours. Cool in pan. Turn out, and scrape off any fat and juices on outside of loaf.

(Pastry — see next page).

Pastry

2¼ cups sifted all-purpose flour
1 teaspoon salt
¾ cup shortening
Cold milk (about ½ cup)
1 egg white

Combine flour and salt. Cut in shortening. Add milk
to make a stiff dough. Roll out about ¾ of the pastry
to a rectangle about 10 by 16 inches. Turn ham loaf
upside down on sheet of waxed paper. Cover with
pastry sheet, easing it at corners to fit loaf without
folds. Trim edges, allowing pastry to extend about
½ inch beyond edges of loaf. Roll out remaining
pastry for top of loaf to a rectangle about 11 by 6
inches, and trim edges. Invert pastry and loaf onto
baking sheet. Remove waxed paper, and fold edges
of pastry over top of loaf. Moisten edges of top
pastry, and fit over top of loaf, pressing edges down
around sides of loaf. Reroll pastry trimmings and
cut with small fancy cutters to form decorations.
Beat egg white lightly, just until foamy. Brush top
and sides of loaf with egg white. Place pastry cutouts
on top, and brush them with egg white. Bake in hot
oven (425° F.) 35 to 45 minutes, until nicely
browned. Serve warm or cold. (Allow loaf to stand
15 or 20 minutes before slicing, if it is to be served
hot.) *Serves 12.*

CALIFORNIA CHEESE PUFFS

18 slices buttered white bread
12 slices American cheese
1 (4-oz.) can green chili peppers
5 eggs
2½ cups hot milk
½ cup Chablis or other white dinner wine
1 teaspoon salt
3 tablespoons shredded Parmesan cheese

Arrange 6 slices bread in bottom of a large buttered pan, about 13 by 9 by 2 inches. Top each slice with a slice of cheese, then another slice of bread and another layer of cheese, sandwich fashion. Drain chili peppers and chop fine. Spoon evenly on top slice of cheese on each sandwich; cover with remaining bread slices. Beat eggs and combine with milk, wine, and salt. Pour over sandwiches; sprinkle with Parmesan cheese. Cover and refrigerate several hours before baking. Bake in a slow oven (325° F.) about 50 to 60 minutes. Serve at once, garnished with sliced tomatoes and canned, drained artichoke hearts, if desired. *Serves 6.*

OLD WORLD VEAL

1½ pounds thin veal steak
¼ cup sifted flour
¾ teaspoon garlic salt
¼ teaspoon seasoned pepper
⅛ teaspoon oregano
1 egg, beaten
¼ cup light cream
⅓ cup fine cracker crumbs
⅓ cup shredded Parmesan cheese
1 tablespoon finely chopped parsley
2 tablespoons olive oil
1 tablespoon butter
¾ cup white dinner wine

Cut veal into serving-size pieces. Dip each piece in flour mixed with garlic salt, pepper, and oregano, then in egg beaten with cream. Dip again in cracker crumbs mixed with cheese and parsley. Brown slowly on both sides in heated oil and butter (add 1 more tablespoon butter, if necessary, toward end of browning). Remove meat to baking pan or oven-proof baking dish. Add wine to drippings left in pan; stir and bring to a boil; pour over meat. Cover and bake in a moderately hot oven (400° F.) until veal is tender, about 35 minutes. Serve with hot buttered noodles, if desired. *Serves 6.*

POTATO PUFF

¼ cup butter or margarine
3 cups mashed potatoes
2 eggs
¾ cup undiluted evaporated milk
¼ cup Chablis or other white dinner wine
1 teaspoon salt
1 teaspoon grated onion
4 to 6 slices bacon, cooked crisp and crumbled
½ cup grated American cheese

Melt butter and blend into potatoes. Beat eggs;
combine with milk, wine, salt, and onion; add to
potatoes and beat until well blended. Stir in
crumbled bacon. Turn into lightly buttered casserole
and top with grated cheese. Bake until puffed and
golden brown in a moderately slow oven (325° F.)
about 45 to 50 minutes. Serve at once. *Serves 6.*

SOUR CREAM CABBAGE

3 tablespoons butter or margarine
1 clove garlic, minced
8 cups finely shredded cabbage, packed
¼ cup Chablis or other white dinner wine
1 egg, beaten
⅓ cup dairy sour cream
1 tablespoon lemon juice
1 tablespoon sugar
1½ teaspoons salt
½ teaspoon celery seed

Melt butter in large skillet. Cook garlic in butter slightly, over low heat. Add cabbage and wine; simmer, covered, 8 to 15 minutes, or until tender. Combine remaining ingredients. Add to cabbage; toss and serve. *Serves 4-6.*

236

VEAL ARTICHOKE

2 cloves garlic
Oil (half olive oil, if preferred)
2 pounds veal round (flattened to $\frac{1}{4}$ inch
  thickness)
Flour seasoned with salt and pepper
1 (1-lb.) can solid-pack tomatoes
$\frac{1}{2}$ cup Sauterne
$\frac{1}{4}$ teaspoon oregano
2 (10-oz.) packages frozen artichoke hearts

In a heavy skillet, sauté garlic in oil. Dust veal with
seasoned flour; brown in oil. Add tomatoes, wine,
and oregano; mix well. Add frozen artichoke hearts.
Cover; simmer 45 minutes to 1 hour, or until meat
is tender. Serve with steamed rice, tossed green
salad, French bread, and fresh fruit dessert. *Serves 6.*

STUFFED PATTYPAN SQUASH

5 or 6 large pattypan squash
1 medium onion, chopped
2 tablespoons bacon drippings
$\frac{1}{4}$ cup crumbled cooked bacon
$\frac{1}{2}$ teaspoon salt
$\frac{1}{4}$ teaspoon coarsely ground pepper
$\frac{1}{4}$ teaspoon dried basil
Butter
$\frac{1}{2}$ cup Chablis or other white dinner wine
Bacon curls for garnish

Wash squash; remove stem ends. Scoop out centers of
squash and dice fine. Cook onion lightly in bacon
drippings; add diced squash and cook 5 minutes. Add
crumbled bacon, salt, pepper, and basil. Spoon into
squash shells; dot each with butter. Arrange in a
single layer in buttered baking pan or shallow
casserole. Pour wine over squash. Cover and bake
in a moderate oven (350° F.) for 30 minutes, or until
squash is tender. Remove cover the last 5 minutes
to lightly brown tops. Garnish each with a bacon
curl, if desired. *Serves 5–6.*

BAKED CELERY SAUTERNE

1 head celery
1 cup water
½ cup Sauterne
Salt
3 tablespoons butter or margarine
3 tablespoons flour
¾ cup canned consommé or bouillon-cube broth
Pepper
⅓ cup grated Parmesan cheese
Paprika

Trim root end and leaves from celery. Separate
stalks and scrub thoroughly under cold running
water. Scrape outer stalks with a vegetable parer or
a sharp knife to remove coarse fiber. Cut stalks in
2-inch lengths, splitting wide stalks in half. Place
water, wine, and salt in a saucepan and heat to
boiling; add celery; cover and cook for 15 to 20
minutes, or until celery is tender. Drain, reserving
liquid. Arrange celery in a greased shallow baking
dish (10 by 6 by 2 inches is a good size). Melt butter
and stir in flour; add consommé and ½ cup of the
reserved celery liquid; cook, stirring constantly,
until mixture boils and thickens. Season to taste
with salt and pepper. Pour sauce over celery;
sprinkle with grated Parmesan cheese and dust with
paprika. Bake in a moderately hot oven (400° F.) for
about 20 minutes, or until bubbly and brown.
Serves 6.

ZUCCHINI VINAIGRETTE

2 tablespoons finely chopped green pepper
2 tablespoons finely chopped parsley
2 green onions, finely chopped
1 pimiento, finely chopped
1 clove garlic, crushed
3 tablespoons sweet pickle relish
½ cup salad oil
¼ cup wine vinegar
1 teaspoon salt
2 teaspoons sugar
¼ cup white table wine
5 or 6 long slender zucchini

Combine all ingredients except zucchini, mixing
well. Cut ends from zucchini, but do not peel. Cut
into lengthwise strips, about 6 strips to each
zucchini. Cook in boiling salted water for about 3
minutes. Don't overcook. Drain and arrange in wide
bowl or pan. Pour the wine mixture over the
zucchini. Marinate several hours. Serve as cold
vegetable or on salad greens with marinade in
separate bowl. *Serves 4.*

CALIFORNIA CHICKEN BAKE

2 cups chicken broth
1 cup rice
1 teaspoon salt
$\frac{1}{2}$ cup chopped onion
2 tablespoons oil or chicken fat
1 (1-lb.) can tomatoes
$\frac{1}{2}$ cup Chablis
1 teaspoon chili powder
$\frac{3}{4}$ teaspoon salt
1 cup diced cooked chicken
$\frac{1}{4}$ cup chopped canned green chili peppers
  (optional)
$\frac{1}{2}$ cup grated Cheddar cheese

Heat chicken broth to boiling, stir in rice and 1 teaspoon salt, cover and simmer about 20 minutes, until rice is tender and liquid is evaporated. Meanwhile, cook onion in oil or chicken fat until transparent and lightly browned. Add tomatoes, wine, chili powder, and remaining salt, and boil rapidly 15 to 20 minutes, until slightly thickened. Stir in green chili peppers. In baking dish, arrange layers of rice, chicken, and tomato sauce. Top with cheese. Bake in moderate oven (350° F.) about 15 minutes, until cheese is melted and casserole is thoroughly heated. *Serves 4.*

SPOONBREAD WITH SEAFOOD

1½ cups milk
1 cup corn kernels
2 teaspoons sugar
½ teaspoon salt
2 tablespoons butter
⅓ cup uncooked yellow corn meal
2 eggs, separated
½ cup Sauterne

Measure 1 cup milk, corn, sugar, salt, and butter into a medium-size saucepan. Bring to a boil; slowly stir in corn meal. Cook gently, stirring often, for about 5 minutes; mixture will be very thick. Remove from heat and add egg yolks beaten with the remaining ½ cup cold milk and wine. Stir until mixture is well blended. Fold in stiffly beaten egg whites. Pour into a buttered casserole, about 1½ quart capacity. Bake in a slow-moderate oven (325° F.) about 50 minutes, or until spoonbread is a rich golden brown and "set" in the center. Serve at once with Creamed Seafood (below). *Serves 6.*

Creamed Seafood: Melt 3 tablespoons butter in a saucepan. Blend in ¼ cup sifted flour, ¾ teaspoon seasoned salt, ⅛ teaspoon each paprika and curry powder. Slowly add 1½ cups rich milk. Bring to a boil, lower heat and cook, stirring, until thickened and smooth. Add 2 tablespoons finely chopped green or mild onion, 2 teaspoons lemon juice, ½ cup Sauterne or other white dinner wine, 1 cup cooked vegetables such as peas or carrots, and 1 (6½ or 7-oz.) can tuna, drained and flaked. Continue cooking a few minutes longer until thoroughly heated. Serve over spoonbread. If desired, crab, shrimp, lobster, or other seafood may be used in place of tuna.

LEEK QUICHE

2 bunches leeks
$\frac{1}{4}$ cup butter or margarine
1 tablespoon flour
$1\frac{1}{4}$ teaspoons salt
$\frac{1}{8}$ teaspoon nutmeg
$\frac{1}{8}$ teaspoon pepper
1 cup whipping cream
$\frac{1}{3}$ cup Sauterne
3 eggs, beaten
1 pre-baked (9-inch) quiche shell
$\frac{1}{4}$ cup grated Swiss cheese

Cut leeks in thin slices, including tender part of tops (should be about $3\frac{1}{2}$ cups sliced leeks). Cook slowly in butter 20 to 25 minutes, or until tender. Stir in flour, salt, and spices. Add cream, and cook, stirring, until mixture boils. Remove from heat and stir in Sauterne and eggs. Turn into quiche shell, and sprinkle with cheese. Bake in moderately hot oven (375° F.) 25 to 30 minutes, or until set in center and lightly browned on top. Cool slightly before cutting. *Serves 6.*

COMPANY CASSEROLE

1 (8-oz.) package noodles
$\frac{1}{2}$ cup chopped green onion
$\frac{1}{4}$ cup chopped green pepper
$\frac{1}{4}$ cup chopped celery
$\frac{1}{4}$ cup butter or margarine
$\frac{1}{3}$ cup sifted flour
1 teaspoon seasoned salt
$2\frac{1}{2}$ cups chicken broth
$\frac{1}{2}$ cup white dinner wine
$\frac{1}{2}$ cup heavy cream
1 (4-oz.) can mushrooms, undrained
2 ($6\frac{1}{2}$- or 7-oz.) cans tuna
1 small tomato
Cheese Crumbs (recipe below)

Cook noodles in boiling salted water just until
tender; drain well. Cook onion, green pepper, and
celery in butter or margarine just until soft.
Blend in flour and salt. Slowly stir in broth. Cook,
stirring, until sauce boils and thickens. Add wine,
then cream. Add undrained mushrooms and drained
tuna. Combine with cooked drained noodles. Turn
into buttered casserole or baking pan. Bake in a
moderately hot oven (375° F.) 25 minutes. Cut
tomato into small wedges. Arrange in center of
casserole; sprinkle Cheese Crumbs around outer
edge. Bake 10 minutes longer. Garnish with
additional mushrooms, if desired. Let casserole stand
5 to 10 minutes before serving. *Serves 8.*

Cheese Crumbs: Combine $1\frac{1}{2}$ cups soft bread
crumbs with 2 tablespoons melted butter and $\frac{1}{4}$
cup grated American cheese.

244

HOT EGG AND POTATO SALAD

2 strips bacon
3 green onions, chopped
1 cup chopped celery
1 teaspoon flour
½ teaspoon dry mustard
1¼ teaspoons salt
⅓ cup Sauterne
1 tablespoon white wine vinegar
2 cups diced boiled potato
6 hard-cooked eggs, diced
2 tablespoons chopped parsley
2 tablespoons chopped pimiento
1 cup grated Cheddar cheese

Cook bacon until crisp. Remove bacon; crumble and
set aside. Cook onion and celery in bacon fat until
soft but not browned. Stir in flour, mustard, salt, and
wine, and cook and stir until mixture boils. Blend in
wine vinegar. Pour over potato and eggs; add
bacon, parsley, and pimiento; and mix lightly. Turn
into shallow baking dish and top with cheese. Bake
in moderately hot oven (375° F.) for 15 to 20
minutes, until salad is heated and cheese is melted.
Serves 4 to 6.

CHEESE SALAD RING

1 envelope unflavored gelatin
$\frac{1}{4}$ cup white dinner wine
1 cup heavy cream, whipped
1 cup milk
$\frac{1}{2}$ teaspoon paprika
Salt
$1\frac{1}{4}$ cups grated American or Cheddar cheese

Soften gelatin in wine for 5 minutes; dissolve over hot water. Blend whipped cream, milk, dissolved gelatin, paprika, and salt; chill. When mixture begins to thicken, fold in cheese. Pour into an oiled 1-quart ring mold or 6 (5-oz.) individual ring molds; chill until firm. Unmold on crisp salad greens and fill center with diced pineapple, orange or grapefruit sections, quartered tomatoes, or any desired fruit or vegetable. Serve with French dressing. *Serves 6.*

CURRIED TURKEY IN SPINACH RING

1 medium-sized onion, minced
¼ cup butter or margarine
⅓ cup flour
1 teaspoon curry powder
1 cup chicken or turkey broth
½ cup California Sauterne or other white
   dinner wine
½ cup cream or undiluted evaporated milk
1 tablespoon Sherry
Salt and pepper
2 cups coarsely diced, cooked turkey
1 (4-oz.) can mushroom stems and pieces,
   drained
1 tablespoon chopped parsley

Sauté onion gently in butter for 5 minutes. Blend in flour and curry powder; and stock and Sauterne; cook, stirring constantly, until mixture boils and thickens. Stir in cream, Sherry, salt and pepper. Add turkey, mushrooms and parsley. Heat gently but thoroughly. Serve in the center of Spinach Ring (see next page). *Serves 6.*

SPINACH RING

1 (10-oz.) package frozen chopped spinach
$\frac{1}{4}$ cup butter or margarine
$\frac{1}{4}$ cup flour
1 cup milk
$\frac{1}{2}$ cup grated American cheese
3 eggs, separated
Salt and pepper to taste

Cook spinach according to directions on carton.
Drain *thoroughly*. Melt butter and stir in flour; add
milk and cook, stirring constantly, until mixture
boils and thickens. Add cheese and stir until melted.
Remove from heat. Add spinach and slightly beaten
egg yolks. Season with salt and pepper. Fold in
stiffly beaten egg whites. Pour into a well-greased
8$\frac{1}{2}$-inch (1$\frac{1}{4}$-quart) ring mold; set in a shallow pan
of hot water. Bake in a moderately hot oven (375°)
about 45 minutes, or until firm. Remove from oven
and let stand a few minutes before unmolding
on a heated platter. Fill center with Curried Turkey
(page 247). *Serves 6.*

ORANGE-MARSHMALLOW FREEZE

1 pound marshmallows
2 cups orange juice
½ cup California Sauterne or other white
   dinner wine
¼ cup lemon juice
Dash of salt

Set refrigerator control at coldest setting. Combine
all ingredients in a double boiler. Heat over boiling
water until marshmallows are melted and ingredients
are well blended, stirring frequently. Cool. Turn
into refrigerator freezing tray. Freeze until frozen 1
inch from side of tray. Turn into a chilled bowl; beat
with a rotary beater until smooth. Return to tray;
freeze until firm. *Serves 6.*

SAUTERNE VELVET PIE

1 (3-oz.) package orange or lemon gelatin
½ cup hot water
¼ cup orange juice
½ cup Sauterne
1 (8-oz.) package cream cheese
2 teaspoons lemon juice
4 to 5 tablespoons sugar
1 cup whipping cream
1 (9-inch) pie shell, baked

Stir gelatin, water, and orange juice together. Heat, stirring, until gelatin dissolves. Add wine and cool. Beat cream cheese until smooth with lemon juice and sugar. Slowly beat in gelatin mixture; chill until mixture begins to thicken. Beat cream until stiff, then quickly beat into the wine gelatin. Turn into baked pie shell and chill until firm. *Serves 6 to 8.*

SLAW-FILLED TOMATOES

4 large firm tomatoes, chilled
3 cups finely shredded crisp cabbage
½ cup grated carrot
¾ cup Sauterne Dressing

Rinse tomatoes; cut thin slice from top of each removing stem ends. Hollow tomatoes leaving about ½ inch rim. Turn upside down to drain. Combine cabbage, carrot and dressing. Spoon into tomato shells. *Serves 4.*

SAUTERNE DRESSING

2 tablespoons flour
2 tablespoons sugar
3 tablespoons salad oil
1 tablespoon seasoned salt
1 tablespoon dry mustard
½ cup Sauterne, Chablis or other white wine
½ cup water
⅓ cup wine vinegar
2 eggs, lightly beaten

Thoroughly combine flour, sugar, oil, salt, mustard, wine and water in top of double boiler. Cook and stir over boiling water until mixture thickens. Combine vinegar and beaten eggs; stir in about ½ cup of the hot sauce. Stir egg mixture very slowly into sauce in double boiler. Cook over hot water, stirring constantly, until mixture thickens and mounds. Remove from heat at once and pour into bowl or jar. Cool, then refrigerate. *Makes 1¾ cups.*

SOUR CREAM-CHILE MACARONI

½ cup chopped green onion
¼ cup butter or margarine
⅔ cup sifted all-purpose flour
1½ teaspoons salt
2 cups rich milk
½ cup Sauterne, Chablis or other
   white dinner wine
½ to 1 cup aged Cheddar cheese
1 (4-oz.) can green chile, chopped
1 (1-lb.) package macaroni, cooked
1 cup (½ pint) commercial sour cream

Cook onion in butter until soft but not browned.
Blend in flour and salt. Slowly stir in milk. Cook,
stirring, until mixture begins to thicken; add
wine and continue cooking until sauce is thick and
smooth, about 5 minutes. Add cheese and chile,
stirring to blend. Combine sauce with hot cooked
macaroni. Turn into serving dish and top with sour
cream. Garnish the casserole with fresh tomato slices
and a few ripe olives, if desired. *Serves 6.*

CHIPPER MEAT BALLS WITH MUSHROOM SAUCE

1 pound ground beef
1 cup finely crushed potato chips
1 cup milk
1 egg, well beaten
1 tablespoon minced onion
$\frac{1}{2}$ teaspoon salt
$\frac{1}{4}$ teaspoon pepper
3 tablespoons bacon drippings or other fat
1 can condensed cream of mushroom soup
$\frac{1}{2}$ cup Sauterne, Rhine or other white
   dinner wine
$\frac{1}{2}$ cup cream or undiluted evaporated milk

Place beef, potato chips, milk, egg, onion, salt and pepper in a mixing bowl. Mix thoroughly with a wooden spoon or, better still, with your hands. Shape into balls, using about a tablespoonful of the mixture for each one. Heat bacon drippings in a large, heavy skillet and brown balls nicely on all sides. Remove balls from skillet and pour off all but 2 to 3 tablespoons of the pan drippings. Place mushroom soup, wine and cream in skillet; blend well, then add meat balls. Bring to a boil, cover tightly, and simmer gently for 25 minutes, stirring occasionally. Serve with rice, noodles, or mashed potatoes. (Note: These can be prepared ahead of time and reheated in a double boiler, or in a covered casserole in the oven, before serving.) *Serves 4.*

ZUCCHINI-SAUSAGE TORTA

2 pounds zucchini
¾ pound bulk pork sausage
¼ cup chopped onion
½ cup cracker crumbs
2 eggs, lightly beaten
¼ cup white wine
¼ teaspoon mixed Italian herbs
⅛ teaspoon pepper
½ teaspoon monosodium glutamate
⅓ cup grated Parmesan cheese

Cook whole zucchini in boiling, salted water about 15 minutes, or just until tender. Drain and chop coarsely. Cook sausage until almost done; drain off fat. Cook onion slightly in same pan, pushing sausage to sides of pan. Add zucchini and all remaining ingredients, reserving 2 tablespoons cheese for topping. Turn into greased 9-inch pie plate. Sprinkle with remaining cheese. Bake in moderate oven (350 degrees) about 30 to 40 minutes, or until firm and lightly browned. Cut into wedges to serve. Serve hot. *Serves 6 to 8.*

SHRIMP-STUFFED VEGETABLES

3 medium-large zucchini (or similar type squash)
3 medium-large tomatoes
3 tablespoons butter or margarine
$\frac{1}{3}$ cup sifted all-purpose flour
$\frac{1}{2}$ teaspoon salt
$1\frac{1}{4}$ cups rich milk
$\frac{1}{3}$ cup Sauterne or other white wine
1 cup cooked shrimp (or prawns, crab or
    lobster)
2 tablespoons chopped green onion
3 tablespoons grated Parmesan or Cheddar
    cheese

Parboil zucchini until barely tender; trim off ends
and remove part of centers leaving a shell. Skin
tomatoes, if desired, by dipping them in boiling
water a few seconds, then stripping off the skin. (Or,
leave skins on, if preferred.) Remove core and part
of centers leaving a shell. Melt butter, blend in
flour and salt. Stir in milk; cook, stirring until
mixture is quite thick. Add wine, shrimp and onion
and cook a few minutes longer. Fill vegetables with
sauce; sprinkle cheese over top. Bake in a shallow
pan or baking dish in a hot oven (425 degrees) until
heated and vegetables are tender, about 15 to 20
minutes. If desired, vegetables may be served with
a seasoned white or cheese sauce. *Serves 6.*

Cooking with Rosé

SAUCY SHRIMP

¼ cup Rosé
¼ cup peanut oil
1 tablespoon wine vinegar
1 teaspoon instant minced onion
Dash of garlic powder
¼ teaspoon dried dill
½ teaspoon seasoned salt
⅛ teaspoon Tabasco sauce
2 (4½-oz.) cans deveined shrimp, drained
⅓ cup catsup

Combine all ingredients except the catsup, stirring gently to blend. Marinate several hours. When ready to serve stir in catsup. Serve in a bowl surrounded with small toast rounds. *Makes 2 cups.*

SHRIMP SAUCE

¼ cup butter
¼ cup sifted flour
1 cup rich chicken broth
¼ cup Rosé
½ cup light cream
1 egg yolk
¼ pound cleaned, cooked shrimp
Salt

Melt butter; blend in flour. Add chicken broth and cook, stirring constantly, until mixture boils and thickens. Blend in wine. Combine cream with egg yolk; mix well and stir into sauce. Cook, stirring frequently, over low heat for 3 minutes (do not boil). Add shrimp, and salt to taste. Serve over cooked green beans, asparagus, or other green vegetable. *Serves 6.*

SHRIMP CREOLE IN PEPPER CASES

⅓ cup chopped celery
⅓ cup chopped onion
⅓ cup chopped green pepper
1 clove garlic, mashed or chopped
¼ cup butter or shortening
1½ cups raw rice
1 teaspoon salt
1 cup Rosé
1 (10½-oz.) can chicken broth
1 (No. 303) can stewed tomatoes or tomato juice
Dash or two of Tabasco sauce
½ cup shredded Parmesan cheese
1 to 2 cups cleaned, cooked shrimp
6 large green peppers

Cook celery, onion, green pepper, and garlic in
butter in a skillet over moderate heat until
vegetables are soft but not browned. Stir in rice;
sauté about 5 minutes, stirring now and then. Add
salt, wine, broth, and tomatoes; add Tabasco sauce,
if desired, and stir to blend. Cover tightly and cook
over moderately low heat about 15 to 20 minutes.
Stir mixture once or twice during cooking. Before
rice is completely cooked, remove cover and gently
stir in cheese and shrimp. Remove from heat.

In the meantime, wash 6 large green peppers; cut a
thin slice from stem end and remove seeds. Cover
with boiling water and simmer 4 or 5 minutes;
remove and drain peppers upside down. Spoon rice
mixture into pepper cases. Top with additional
cheese, if desired. Place peppers in a baking pan
with ½ inch hot water in bottom. Bake in a
moderately hot oven (375° F.) about 20 minutes.
Serves 6.

GRILLED LOBSTER TAILS

8 frozen rock lobster tails
⅓ cup melted butter
¼ cup Rosé
½ teaspoon seasoned salt

Thaw tails. Cut away and remove underside
membrane. Bend tails back far enough to crack
them so they won't curl while cooking. Place
lobster tails on broiler pan, shell side up.
Broil 4 or 5 inches from heat for 3 minutes. Turn
and brush meat liberally with mixture of butter,
wine, and seasoning. Continue broiling until meat
is tender and looks opaque, about 3 or 4 minutes
longer. Brush again with any remaining butter
mixture. Serve 2 tails to each person, when served
as the main course. *Serves 4.*

ROSY CHICKEN BARBECUE

¼ cup butter or margarine
1 teaspoon cornstarch
1 teaspoon garlic salt
½ teaspoon paprika
½ teaspoon powdered marjoram
¾ cup Rosé
3 broiling chickens, halved

Melt butter, and blend in cornstarch and seasonings.
Add Rosé, and cook, stirring, until mixture thickens
slightly. Place chicken halves, skin side down over
glowing coals, and broil until slightly browned.
Turn, and brush with Rosé mixture. Continue
cooking, turning and brushing frequently, until
chickens are well browned and cooked through.
(Note: This sauce may also be used for broiling
chickens in the oven. The slightly thickened sauce
holds onto the meat better than a straight wine
mixture.) *Serves 6.*

ROAST GOOSE

1 (10-lb.) goose
1 large onion
1 large tart apple
1 cup Rosé
2 tablespoons wine vinegar
2 tablespoons honey
1 tablespoon soy sauce
½ teaspoon powdered sage
¼ teaspoon onion salt
¼ cup red currant or cranberry jelly
Salt and pepper

Prepare goose for roasting, placing peeled and
halved onion and halved apple in body cavity; truss
or skewer to hold shape. Prick fatty surface of goose
with tines of a fork. Beat wine, vinegar, honey, soy,
sage, onion salt, and jelly together until smooth.
Pour over goose and marinate several hours, turning
3 or 4 times. Drain and save marinade. Place goose
in shallow baking pan. Roast in a very hot oven
(500° F.) for ½ hour. Drain off and discard fat which
accumulates in pan. Salt and pepper goose well.
Spoon a little wine marinade over goose. Return to a
moderate oven (350° F.) and continue roasting until
tender, about 3 hours longer. Baste at frequent
intervals with the wine marinade and rich drippings
which collect in the pan. Remove goose to hot
serving platter; keep warm while making gravy.
Skim all excess fat from pan liquid and discard.
Correct seasoning, if needed. Serve the pan liquid
as thin gravy or thicken slightly with a little
cornstarch mixed with cold water. (Note: Giblets
from goose may be simmered until tender in
seasoned water with 1 large onion and 2 stalks
celery. Drain and discard vegetables. Chop giblets
and use along with cooking liquid when making
gravy.) *Serves 4.*

VEAL STEAK ROSÉ

1½ pounds veal steak
2 tablespoons flour
¾ teaspoon garlic salt
¼ teaspoon basil
3 tablespoons cooking oil
¾ cup Rosé
⅓ cup dairy sour cream
⅓ cup grated Parmesan cheese

Cut steak into serving pieces; dredge with flour
mixed with salt and basil. Brown meat on both sides
in heated oil; drain off any excess fat. Add wine to
meat; cover and simmer until meat is tender, about
35 to 40 minutes. Combine sour cream and cheese;
spoon over meat and continue cooking 5 to 10
minutes longer. Remove meat to serving platter, stir
pan juices to blend and serve over meat. *Serves 4.*

CHINESE COCONUT-PEPPER STEAK

1 pound sirloin tips or top round
½ teaspoon monosodium glutamate
2 medium-size green peppers
2 tablespoons salad oil
½ teaspoon salt
⅛ teaspoon pepper
1 clove garlic, cut in half
¾ cup shredded coconut
½ cup beef broth or stock
1 teaspoon sugar
2 tablespoons cornstarch
2 tablespoons soy sauce
⅓ cup Rosé
Hot cooked rice

Slice meat across grain into thin strips about 1 inch long and ½ inch wide. Sprinkle with monosodium glutamate; let stand while preparing rest of ingredients. Slice green pepper diagonally into strips about ¼ inch wide. Heat oil in large frying pan. Add salt, pepper, and garlic. Remove garlic when brown. Add meat slices and sauté 2 minutes, stirring constantly. Remove meat. If necessary, add a little more oil, and in same pan, sauté green pepper for several minutes. Push to one side and sauté coconut for 1 minute. Return beef to pan. Mix broth, sugar, cornstarch, soy sauce, and wine; add to frying pan. Cook, stirring, until liquid thickens. Serve at once with cooked rice. *Serves 4.*

CHILLED HAM SOUFFLÉ

½ cup Rosé
½ cup chicken broth
1 envelope unflavored gelatin
3 eggs, separated
¼ cup dairy sour cream
2 tablespoons finely chopped pimiento
1 teaspoon prepared mustard
Dash of Tabasco sauce
2 cups ground cooked ham
¼ teaspoon salt
¼ teaspoon cream of tartar

Combine Rosé, chicken broth, and gelatin in top of
double boiler, and let stand 5 minutes to soften
gelatin. Heat over hot water. Beat egg yolks lightly.
Stir slowly into hot wine mixture. Cook and stir
until mixture thickens slightly and coats spoon.
Remove from heat and cool slightly. Stir in sour
cream, pimiento, mustard, Tabasco, and ham. Cool
until slightly thickened. Beat egg whites with salt
and cream of tartar until stiff. Fold gently into ham
mixture. Chill a few minutes, until mixture mounds
on a spoon. Fold a long strip of foil in half
lengthwise, and place around a 3-cup soufflé dish to
form a collar. Tie in place with string. Heap soufflé
mixture into dish, and chill until firm. Remove
foil collar just before serving. *Serves 4–6.*

GLAZED CHICKEN ROSÉ

4 or 5 boned chicken breasts
Salt
Pepper
3 tablespoons butter or oil
$\frac{1}{2}$ cup thickly sliced green onion
$1\frac{1}{2}$ tablespoons cornstarch
1 cup chicken broth
$\frac{1}{3}$ cup Rosé
2 teaspoons soy sauce
$\frac{1}{2}$ cup cooked peas
1 can (5 oz.) water chestnuts, halved
Hot buttered spaghetti

Sprinkle chicken breasts with salt and pepper.
Brown slowly in 2 tablespoons butter or oil. Bake at
350 degrees for 20 minutes, until cooked through.
Meanwhile, sauté green onion lightly in remaining
tablespoon oil. Stir in cornstarch; add broth and
Rosé. Pour sauce over chicken and spaghetti to
serve. *Serves 4 or 5.*

MEATBALL STROGANOFF

1 pound ground lean beef
1 egg, lightly beaten
$\frac{1}{2}$ cup soft bread crumbs
1 tablespoon instant minced onion
1 teaspoon salt
$\frac{1}{8}$ teaspoon pepper
$\frac{3}{4}$ cup Rosé
2 tablespoons oil
$1\frac{1}{2}$ cups sliced fresh brown mushrooms
2 tablespoons flour
$\frac{1}{2}$ cup water
1 beef bouillon cube
1 tablespoon tomato paste
$\frac{1}{8}$ teaspoon dry mustard
$\frac{1}{8}$ teaspoon dill weed
$\frac{1}{2}$ cup yogurt

Combine beef, egg, bread crumbs, onion, salt, pepper, and $\frac{1}{4}$ cup Rosé, and mix well. Shape into balls about $1\frac{1}{2}$ inches in diameter. Brown in heated oil, shaking pan to keep them round. Remove meatballs as they are browned. Add mushrooms, and brown lightly. Stir flour into drippings in pan. Add water, bouillon cube, remaining $\frac{1}{2}$ cup Rosé, tomato paste, mustard, and dill. Stir until sauce boils and thickens. Return meatballs to skillet; cover and simmer 10 minutes. Add yogurt, and heat but do not boil. Serve at once, over hot buttered tagliarini or noodles. *Serves 4–5.*

SPRING VEGETABLE SUPPER

½ cup Rosé
½ cup wine vinegar
1½ cups salad oil
1 teaspoon garlic salt
1 teaspoon salt
¼ teaspoon pepper
2 teaspoons dry mustard
1 teaspoon paprika
Assorted cooked vegetables such as:
   2 dozen asparagus stalks
   3 cups cut yellow or green beans
   2 cups sliced carrots
3 large (or 6 small) firm tomatoes, sliced,
   quartered, or cut in flower shapes
Avocado-Shrimp Dressing (recipe below)

Combine wine, vinegar, oil, and dry seasonings in a
quart jar. Cover and shake vigorously until well
blended; pour over vegetables. Cover and chill
several hours. When ready to serve, drain and
arrange on chilled serving platter. Serve with
Avocado-Shrimp Dressing. Crisp greens may
accompany the vegetables, if desired, or vegetable
platter may be served with cold meats, chicken, or
turkey. *Serves 6.*

Avocado-Shrimp Dressing: Pour ¼ cup Rosé over
1 cup deveined cooked shrimp. Cover and refrigerate
several hours. Then mash coarsely or chop shrimp
(do not drain). Cut 1 small avocado in half, remove
seed and skin, and mash fruit. Blend with 1 cup
dairy sour cream (half mayonnaise may be used,
if desired), 1 teaspoon dry mustard, ⅛ teaspoon
dried dill, ½ teaspoon salt, and ½ cup grated
pared cucumber; add shrimp mixture. Cover and
chill. *Makes about 2½ cups.*

CRAB LOUIS IN ASPIC

2 envelopes plain gelatin
1¼ cups cold water
¾ cup chili sauce
⅔ cup Rosé
½ cup dairy sour cream
1 tablespoon minced green onion
½ teaspoon dried dill
¾ teaspoon salt
1 tablespoon lemon juice
1 (2½-oz.) can sliced ripe olives
4 hard-cooked eggs
1½ cups fresh or canned crab meat

Soften gelatin in ½ cup cold water. Heat chili sauce
and remaining ¾ cup water. Add gelatin, stirring
until dissolved. Remove from heat and stir in the
wine, sour cream, onion, dill, salt and lemon juice.
Chill until mixture thickens. Drain olives. Set aside
a few of the olive slices for garnish. Cut 2 of the
eggs into wedges or slices for garnish. Chop
remaining two eggs and add to gelatin with remaining
olive slices and crab. Turn into lightly oiled 6-cup
mold or into small molds. Chill firm. Unmold on
salad greens. Garnish with reserved egg and olive
slices. *Makes 8 to 10 servings.*

WINE-BUTTER GLAZED PEACHES

3 tablespoons butter
2 tablespoons lemon juice
6 small peaches, peeled
$\frac{1}{3}$ cup brown sugar
$\frac{1}{3}$ cup Rosé
$\frac{1}{2}$ cup heavy cream

Melt butter in large skillet. Add lemon juice and peaches. Turn fruit to coat with butter. Sprinkle with brown sugar and wine. Poach over low heat, turning often, about 15 minutes until heated and lightly glazed. Push peaches to one side and stir in cream. Bring to a boil. Lower heat and simmer rapidly several minutes. Serve peaches warm with some of the pan sauce. *Serves 6.*

FRUIT FREEZE, ROSÉ

1 (1 lb. 4$\frac{1}{2}$-oz.) can crushed pineapple
1$\frac{1}{2}$ cups miniature marshmallows
$\frac{1}{3}$ cup Rosé
2 tablespoons fresh lemon juice
$\frac{1}{4}$ teaspoon salt
2 tablespoons chopped maraschino cherries
2 tablespoons syrup from cherries
$\frac{1}{2}$ cup whipping cream
1 sliced banana
Lettuce cups

Combine pineapple and marshmallows and let stand an hour or longer, until marshmallows are soft and partly melted. Stir in wine, lemon juice, salt, cherries and cherry syrup. Whip cream until stiff. Fold cream and banana into first mixture. Turn into freezing tray and place in freezing compartment until barely firm. Cut into squares or rectangles and serve in lettuce cups. *Makes 6–9 servings.*

ROSÉ FIG WHIP

12 fig newtons
$\frac{1}{4}$ cup Rosé
$\frac{1}{2}$ cup whipping cream
Dash of salt
1 tablespoon sugar
1 tablespoon fresh lemon juice

Dice fig newtons into bowl, and sprinkle wine over them. Let stand until wine is absorbed. Whip cream with salt and sugar until stiff. Blend in lemon juice, and fold in cooky mixture. Chill. *Serves 4.*

ROSÉ MUSHROOM SAUCE

1 cup fresh button mushrooms
2 tablespoons butter or margarine
1 bouillon cube
$1\frac{1}{2}$ teaspoons cornstarch
$\frac{1}{2}$ cup Rosé

Remove stems and wash mushrooms; dry well. Melt butter, crumble in bouillon cube, and add mushrooms; cook gently until almost tender. Blend cornstarch into wine and add to mushrooms; simmer about 5 minutes. Add to $1\frac{1}{2}$ to 2 cups hot cooked vegetables such as peas, green beans, celery, or carrots. *Serves 4-5.*

GLAZED SANDWICHES

1½ cups tomato juice
1 small bay leaf
¾ teaspoon salt
⅛ teaspoon whole cloves
2 tablespoons chopped green onion
⅓ cup chopped celery
1 (3-oz.) package lemon gelatin
2 tablespoons wine vinegar
½ cup Rosé
Open-face appetizer sandwiches (recipes below)

Mix and bring to a boil tomato juice, bay leaf, salt,
cloves, green onion, and celery. Cover and simmer
10 to 15 minutes. Strain; add lemon gelatin to hot
liquid and stir to dissolve. Add vinegar and wine.
Chill until mixture thickens slightly. To glaze,
arrange open-face appetizer sandwiches on cake
rack and slowly spoon or pour slightly thickened
glaze over filling; chill until firm. *Makes 2 cups of
glaze.*

Open-face Sandwiches: Use hard-cooked egg slices,
whole shrimp or crab legs, sliced green olives on
buttered whole wheat or rye bread. Or try smoked
salmon and cream cheese spread on rye bread, or
any of your favorite combinations.

Date-Cheese Sandwiches

Blend 1 (8-oz.) package softened cream cheese with
¼ cup Sherry, ¼ cup chopped mint, and ¼ cup finely
chopped dates. Spread on nut bread or thin slices of
whole wheat bread.

Ham-Cheese Sandwich Spread

Combine equal portions of deviled ham and cream
cheese. Moisten to spreading consistency with
Sauterne or other white dinner wine. Spread on thin
slices of rye bread and cut into dainty sandwiches.

RASPBERRY TART

1 (10-oz.) package frozen raspberries
2 tablespoons cornstarch
2 to 3 tablespoons sugar
$\frac{1}{8}$ teaspoon salt
$\frac{1}{3}$ cup Rosé
6 (3-inch) tart shells, baked
Sweetened whipped cream

Thaw raspberries and drain syrup into saucepan. Combine cornstarch, sugar to taste, and salt; blend well, and stir into raspberry syrup. Cook, stirring constantly, until clear and thickened. Remove from heat and blend in wine. Add drained raspberries and blend lightly. Cool, and spoon into tart shells. Just before serving, top with whipped cream. *Makes 6 tarts.*

FRUIT CUP ROSÉ

$\frac{1}{3}$ cup Rosé
$\frac{1}{3}$ cup sugar
Dash of cloves
Dash of nutmeg
Dash of salt
$\frac{1}{3}$ cup orange juice
1 basket strawberries
2 fresh peaches

Combine wine, sugar, spices, and salt, and heat gently, stirring until sugar is dissolved. Stir in orange juice and cool. Rinse and hull strawberries. Peel and slice peaches. Combine fruits with wine mixture and chill thoroughly. *Serves 6.*

RHUBARB SWIRLS

1½ pounds rhubarb
½ cup Rosé
1 cup sugar
1 tablespoon cornstarch
¼ teaspoon salt
¼ teaspoon cinnamon
1½ cups biscuit mix
½ cup milk
2 tablespoons melted butter or margarine
3 tablespoons sugar

Wash rhubarb, trim off leaves, and cut stalks in
½-inch slices. Turn all but 1 cup into 8½-inch-round
baking dish. Combine wine, 1 cup sugar, cornstarch,
salt, and cinnamon, and pour over rhubarb in dish.
Set in hot oven (400° F.) while preparing swirls.
Combine biscuit mix and milk to make a soft dough.
Turn out onto floured board and roll to rectangle
about 8 by 12 inches. Spread with 1 tablespoon of
the butter. Chop remaining cup rhubarb and
sprinkle over dough. Sprinkle with 2 tablespoons
sugar. Roll up as for jelly roll, to make 12-inch roll.
Cut into 8 slices. Remove rhubarb from oven, and
arrange swirls over it. Brush swirls with remaining
butter, and sprinkle with remaining tablespoon
sugar. Bake about 30 minutes, until swirls are
nicely browned. Serve warm. *Makes 8 swirls.*

ROSÉ WINE JELLY

2 cups Rosé
1 cup bottled cranberry juice cocktail
1 (1³/₄-oz.) package powdered pectin
3¹/₂ cups sugar

Combine Rosé, cranberry juice cocktail, and fruit
pectin in 5- or 6-quart saucepan. Bring to hard boil
over high heat, stirring. Stir in sugar and bring to
full rolling boil. Boil hard 1 minute, stirring
constantly. Remove from heat; skim off foam with
metal spoon. Pour at once into hot sterilized
glasses, leaving ¹/₂ inch space at top. Seal with
paraffin. *Fills 6 6-ounce glasses.*

WINE AND FOOD

*"Champagne with foaming whirls
As white as Cleopatra's melted pearls."*
— Lord Byron

What wine do you serve with Coquille St. Jacques?
With meat loaf? With Brook trout? At a wine
tasting party? At the informal buffet that will
feature many different foods? We all know that
traditionally red wine goes with red meat, white
wine with fish and poultry. (Rosé goes with
everything, and is especially ideal for those dishes
you're uncertain about.) Of course, there are those
who rebel against the dictates of those centuries-old
rules. They say you should drink the wine that
appeals to you, regardless of color.

There is, however, a middle road between the
traditional rules and complete abandon. True, the
most important thing is that you like the wine,
and the combination of the wine with the food. But
consider trying suggested wines with specific dishes;
you may find you've been missing some fantastic
taste experiences. After all, the people who made up
the original rules did so because, from much tasting,
they had been able to match the flavors, the
subtleties of various wines to foods. Using their
recommendations as guidelines, you too can become
an expert — and start experimenting on your own.
But even using the classic guidelines, some dishes
do present problems: spaghetti with meat sauce;
spaghetti with butter and cheese; Veal Parmigiana
with spicy tomato sauce; Veal Milanese with a
simple butter and lemon sauce. But consider these
possibilities. Both spaghetti and veal are essentially

277

bland flavors; the sauce should determine the wine you'll serve. Spaghetti with a savory, spicy tomato-meat sauce fairly demands a flavorful, full-bodied red wine, as does Veal Parmigiana with its zesty sauce and liberal sprinkle of strong cheese. In Italy, which produces its share of fine red wines, Chianti is the appointed wine for these dishes. If you're drinking American, try a California Chianti or an even more robust Barbera or Charbono.

Similarly, for the milder, more subtle flavors of spaghetti in butter sauce or Veal Milanese, a full-flavored white wine such as Chablis or Chardonnay will complement the dish without overwhelming it.

Another problem in matching wine to food is, given so many different wines in both red and white, which red wine do you choose? Which white? Knowing the differences between wines in wine categories helps. For example, Filet Mignon picks up a highly seasoned flavor from Sauce Béarnaise that requires the rich, full flavor of a Burgundy or a California Pinot Noir. (Keep in mind, the relative importance of the occasion, and match the importance of the wine to it. If you're serving Filet Mignon with Sauce Béarnaise it is presumably a very important occasion — hence, a Pinot Noir, rather than the generic Burgundy, would probably be in order.)

Prime Ribs of Beef au jus, no less a delicacy than the Filet, is less seasoned, more subtle, and so should the wine be subtle. This calls for the lighter-bodied Claret or Cabernet Sauvignon or Zinfandel. Matched to the more delicate flavors of the Prime Ribs, the delightful complexities of these wines can be enjoyed to their fullest.

Family dishes for informal suppers are dressed up when they're accompanied by one of the good "jug" wines. Meat loaf, depending on how spicy you make it, can call for a Burgundy or a Claret. The light, fruity Burgundy-type, Gamay Beaujolais, is also a good choice, and is marvelous with the milder-flavored red meats such as lamb and game birds. Beef stew is enhanced by Burgundy, both *in* the stew and *with* it. Try a lighter-bodied Claret with lamb stew.

Ham, depending on how you cook it, can be accompanied by red, white, or Rosé. Glazed and studded with pungent cloves, it would take a light-bodied red, preferably a Zinfandel or Gamay. A roast fresh ham, or loin of pork, requires one of the fuller-bodied whites, a Chablis or Chardonnay. Rosé goes equally well with both, but, as popular as it is, Rosé seems to be "all things to all men." It is indispensable at picnics, where the food may range from barbecued hamburger to hot dogs covered with hot mustard, to macaroni, potato and egg salads requiring an "all-purpose" wine. Served cold, it is the perfect summer wine. (This versatile wine is also the obvious choice for a multi-dished buffet where you only want to serve one wine.)

These above examples give the clue to wine-food marriages. The more highly-seasoned the food is, the more robust the wine should be.

The white wines do present some problems. A very light dish, such as simple broiled-in-butter scallops would be best accompanied by a light, flowery wine such as a Rhine or Riesling, while another popular scallop dish, Coquille St. Jacques, with its rich cream sauce, is most beautifully complemented with the fuller-bodied Pinot Chardonnay (or Chablis — though, here again, Coquille is an important dish, deserving of an important wine).

Here are some typically good food-wine combinations:

FOODS	WINES

Easter Ham

As with any occasion where you have a crowd to please, you will want to choose a wine that will please the majority. Ham, whether fresh or smoked, has a tendency toward sweetness and since the taste of most American wine drinkers also tilts in favor of the sweet, a Sauvignon Blanc or sweet Sauterne would probably be enthusiastically received. However, when unsure, serve the infallible Rosé.

Fettuccini "Alfredo"
(Butter and Cheese sauce)

Lighter white wine, such as Rhine, Riesling or Chablis.

Filet Mignon

If you can afford this, you can also afford the wine which will best complement it, preferably an aged Cabernet or Zinfandel. If you like a lot of Béarnaise sauce, you may prefer a fine Pinot Noir.

Filet of Sole

Whether Almondine or Veronique, this dish is delicate enough to be complemented yet not overwhelmed by a fine Johannisberg Riesling, Traminer or any other light white wine. The same kind of wine will go equally with almost any sea food except for those heavily flavored with a spicy sauce, in which case you might prefer one of the fuller-bodied Chablis-types or even a light-bodied red such as Gamay Beaujolais.

Hamburger and French Fries

Chianti or Burgundy types.

Thanksgiving Turkey	Presumably the Thanksgiving feast will bring together a number of beloved friends, each with a distinctive taste for white meat or dark, mashed potatoes or yams, stuffed celery or creamed onions. Perhaps here is the ideal place for Rosé. You surely can't go wrong! You might want to inject an unexpected bit of pleasure by offering one of the "Crackling Rosés" that have a slight sparkle suggestive of Champagne.
Shrimp Fra Diavolo	Hot and spicy, this food category can include such dishes as Chili Con Carne, Barbecued Beef—even the newly popular Sloppy Joes. It obviously calls for a robust full-flavored wine of the red Burgundy type or a Chianti.
Veal Milanese	Again, a light meat with a tart yet light sauce. This dish calls for a full-bodied white wine—Chablis or, for an important event, a Pinot Chardonnay.
Veal Parmigiana	Light-flavored meat with a full-flavored sauce. This dish can take a wine as robust as Burgundy or as subtle as a Cabernet or a Zinfandel.
Leg of Lamb	Perhaps the one meat dish that cannot be improved and can be most definitely damaged by the use of wine in the cooking is Leg of Lamb. Nothing can quite match the aroma and flavor of Leg of Lamb gravy. However, this magnificent dish can be immeasurably enhanced by a fine, aged red wine of equal subtlety, such as a Cabernet. Many red wine buffs would serve something more robust, such as Pinot Noir.
Prime Ribs au jus	Superb, in their simplicity, Prime Ribs are deserving of the finest, whether you call it Claret, Zinfandel, or America's best Cabernet Sauvignon.

Salisbury Steaks	This faintly disguised hamburger could call for a less full-bodied wine, such as Gamay or Zinfandel.
Sirloin Steak Barbecued	The steak of steaks—lightly charred outside, melting pink inside, this demands the best American Burgundy —the noble Pinot Noir.
Spaghetti with Meat Sauce	A full-flavored dish requiring a strong-flavored wine such as Chianti or Burgundy.

WINE AND CHEESE

"And Noah he often said to his wife when he sat down to dine,
'I don't care where the water goes if it doesn't get into the wine.'"
— G. K. Chesterton

With the growing popularity of the wine and cheese
party, the same question of what wine with what
cheese arises. Here again, the new rule should apply.
You would scarcely serve a delicate Riesling with a
sharp Roquefort. Better with this tangy cheese would
be a really rich, full-flavored Burgundy, Pinot Noir,
or Chianti.

A fine, aged Brie can easily go with the fuller-bodied
whites such as Pinot Chardonnay and Chablis, as
well as the lighter reds—Gamay Beaujolais, Claret,
Cabernet Sauvignon, and Zinfandel. (In the wine
and cheese "match," Rosé wines do not go with
everything. A sharp Cheddar or Roquefort would
drown the taste of a Rosé, and in any case, care
should be taken not to "cop out" of the wine decision
by choosing a Rosé whenever you're not sure which
wine would be appropriate.)

Some outstandingly good wine-cheese combinations:

CHEESE	WINES
American Cheese	Light reds or whites—Zinfandel, Gamay, any of the Rhine, Chablis, or a Rosé.
Boursault	Zinfandel, Claret, Chablis, Chardonnay, Gamay Beaujolais.
Brie	Mild reds such as Beaujolais; more robust whites such as Chardonnay and Chablis.
Camembert	Almost any robust wine. This is a hearty cheese, deserving of an equally hearty wine.
Cheese Dip	Depending on how pungent the mixture, the wine should match it in robustness. Actually, any combination of sour cream and other flavoring can stand up to a fairly full-bodied wine such as Burgundy or Chardonnay. The lighter wines, such as Rhine would be lost.
Monterey Jack	Zinfandel, Claret, Chablis, and Chardonnay.
Port Salut	Zinfandel, Claret—but preferably, because of its mild flavor, one of the whites, such as a Riesling.
Roquefort/Bleu Cheese	Burgundy or Chianti, Pinot Noir.
Sharp Cheddar	Burgundy or Chianti, Pinot Noir.
Swiss Cheese	Any of the Rhines, or Rieslings.
Tilsit	Same as Port Salut, but preferably one of the lighter reds, because of the more robust character of this cheese.

Any of the flavored, mild and slightly sweeter cheese should be served with light, white wines. When wine and cheese make up the whole menu, try some of the sweeter white table wines such as Semillon and Sauvignon Blanc. These wines, unlike the completely dry, full-bodied Chablis types and Chardonnays which fairly cry out for *food,* go very well with canapés and cheese-and-cracker combinations — making the *wine* party a delightfully interesting departure from the usual cocktail party.

SERVING WINE

"If God forbade drinking would he have made wine so good?"
— *Cardinal Richelieu*

Much has been written here and elsewhere about how to appreciate wine, but when the moment of truth arrives — when we actually have to present our choice at our own dinner table — most of us experience an instant of sheer terror. The first shock may come from the realization that we don't at all know why we picked this wine over all others. Too frequently, it was because the price was right and the label attractive. An attractive label is a very good substitute — and often much less expensive — than an attractive wine. An eye for artistic design, however, is *not* a substitute for fine winemaking — or appreciation.

Guests invited to enjoy a wine are completely in your hands; you must lead the way, letting them know what to look for, explaining the pleasures you yourself have discovered. Of course, if you don't know the wine itself, you can hardly describe it to others, which is a good reason for home tastings, an opportunity for you to discover various wines. Forearmed with a knowledge of what you like and why you like it, you need have no fears. If you have taken the trouble to *taste* in order to arrive at a pleasing wine, you may feel secure; your guests are quite likely to applaud your choice.

289

Of course some of your security will be based on the way you *serve* the wine. As with all fine things, there are good-sense rules to the serving of wine:

1. *Open the wine an hour before serving.* With the exception of Champagne, all wines improve if allowed some time to "breathe" so that the splendid blend of aroma, bouquet, and flavor can draw substance from the air. (This might seem to be a contradiction of a previous statement that air is harmful to wine. It *can* be over a prolonged period, since air causes the wine to oxidize and eventually sour. But most wine, after long confinement in the bottle, seems to "bloom" with an hour or so of breathing time after opening.)

A bottle of Sherry to be enjoyed before dinner should be opened an hour or so before guests arrive. The table wines should be opened an hour before they are to be served. In restaurants, it's a good idea to order the wine when you order the meal, with instructions to bring it and open it immediately. While you linger over your aperitifs, the wine will be "growing" to its full potential.

2. *Serve the wine at the proper temperature.* In serving wine at home, you will, of course, chill the whites and Rosés three to four hours before serving. But because cold has a numbing effect on wine, do bring them out an hour before they are to be served; open them; and continue the chilling in an

290

ice bucket* for another half-hour. (You could return the open bottles to the refrigerator, but wine, like butter, tends to pick up flavors from other foods.) At least fifteen minutes before you plan to serve these wines, remove them from the ice completely so that they may warm slightly – the idea is to serve them *chilled,* not iced. (Of course, it's not advisable to keep them sitting around the hot kitchen, either. Since, even if more than one wine is to be served, the white will be the first, put them right on the dining table for all to admire.)

Red wines present a special problem: Everyone knows they should be served at room temperature, but the room temperature in American homes is much too warm for wine. Pre-opened and then lightly stoppered with their own corks, red wines may be stored in the refrigerator for fifteen minutes to bring them down closer to the original meaning of "room temperature." When you take them out, remove the stoppers and let them rest an hour or so until you're ready to pour.

---

*Ice buckets are deceptively named. For greatest utility, they should be called ice-water buckets. Unless you really *want* to do battle with several dozen ice cubes resisting the entrance into their midst of a bottle of wine – you should ⅓ fill the bucket with water; stir several ice cubes around in it for a few moments, and then put in the bottle of wine. The cubes will part like the Red Sea and the wine will chill as thoroughly as if packed in solid ice. (In lieu of an ice bucket, you can always call an ordinary deep "pot" to understudy.)

Champagne, incidentally, is the exception to the above rules. It should be served icy cold and immediately after opening.

3. *Use the proper glasses.* Any department store will be perfectly willing to sell you a complete service of stemware. There are many styles to choose from, some of them excellent, others completely unsatisfactory — including a Sherry glass that resembles a thimble-on-a-stem, and wine glasses widening out to a degree guaranteed to let all the aroma and essence of the wine escape before you ever get near it. The popular Champagne "saucers" are a good example of the ultimate desecration of wine by glass designers. They're pretty to look at, but unwieldy to hold — the only way is to cradle the saucer part in your hand, which warms the Champagne — and the width of the glass is certain to let out the precious bubbles, which are, after all, the main attraction of Champagne.

Ideally, wine glasses should be clear, untinted and without decoration, even etching. This is the only way to display the wine's color to full advantage. (That is not to say you must put away the cut-glass heirloom service that's been in the family for generations. But if you use them, be prepared to have the wine take second place to the glass, at least from a visual standpoint.)

A

Even more ideally, a wine glass should allow for an adequate serving. The "average" (actually the minimum) is 4 ounces. Since a wine glass should never be filled more than two-thirds, it should be large enough to allow room for the aroma and bouquet to gather near the top. You'll need at least a 6-ounce glass. More generous hosts use 8-ounce glasses and let their guests enjoy an extra bonus.

All wine glasses should be shaped so that they balloon out and narrow at the top, in order to capture the fragrances. Most of the reliable glass manufacturers follow this rule. But traditional wine glasses *do* vary in size and shape according to the specific wine.

A. **Rhine wine.** Notice that the glass is tall-stemmed — the stem not only lends beauty, but serves as a "handle" so that our fingers do not touch the wine and warm it — but the bowl is small. Rhine wine usually accompanies the earliest course at dinner — the soup or the fish — and it should prepare your palate for the fuller-bodied wines to come.

B. **Other white wines.** Deep-bowled, with a relatively short stem, this is the glass in which to serve the full white Burgundies and Chablis that complement fowl or light meats. (Rosés may be served in the same glass.)

C. **Red wines.** To provide a generous serving, the bowl of this glass is deep, for red is the final wine of the dinner, except for the Champagne or dessert wine which may follow. The stem is longer than for most whites, but shorter than the Rhine wine glass. The red wine glass announces the importance of the wine by its size and shape.

D. Recently, a "Burgundy balloon" has become popular. Oversized, but beautifully shaped, it makes for a special occasion no matter what wine you serve in it—a priceless Pinot Noir or an informal Cold Duck.

E. **Sherry and Port glasses.** In this category, all of the appetizer and dessert wines are included. Too often, Sherry glasses (as well as those for after-dinner wines) are tiny replicas of cocktail glasses. Filled to the proper 2 to 3 ounces, they offer little room for the enjoyment of the aromatic essences of the wine. If you have it in mind to buy a wine service, unless the bowls of the Sherry glasses have at least a 4-ounce capacity, skip them and use one of the other glasses in their stead.

F. **Champagne.** We have already discussed the disadvantages of the champagne "saucer." Perhaps the best glass for this wine is the champagne "tulip," so named because it does indeed resemble a tulip, curving in towards the top to preserve the natural effervescence of the Champagne. Others seem to resemble a smaller version of the "Pilsner" glass for beer. In any case, the elongated shape helps keep the bubbles alive.

G. **The all-purpose glass.** Designed somewhat in
the shape of a tulip, this glass has become
increasingly popular – and deservedly so. It has all
the advantages of each of the glasses described
above, so it is perfectly suitable to all wines. It has
the tulip shape so important to Champagne and to
the fragrances of other wines; it is long stemmed for
both beauty and utility; it has a 9-ounce capacity,
which allows a generous serving and proper space
to enjoy the fragrances.

The all-purpose glass is an important development, allowing those who enjoy wine to indulge their taste for the beverage itself rather than the elaborate trappings which surround it. For much less than it would cost you to assemble a complete wine service, you may obtain enough all-purpose glasses to see you through a multi-course meal for eight or more.

4. *The order of serving.* A problem arises only when you have more than one wine to serve. In general, as shown in the drawing, the wine glass is placed on the outside of the water goblet. Should you be serving two wines, the white wine glass should be placed in front of the red wine glass, at a right angle to the water goblet. This is reasonable, since the white wine will come first, along with the lighter fish or soup that will precede the heartier portion of the meal. As the white wine is finished, the glass is removed, leaving the red wine glass in its proper place next to the water goblet.

Order of Serving

Water
goblet

Red wine

White
wine

Leftover Wine

Being a generous host, you have thoughtfully
provided more than enough of everything for your
guests and there are leftovers. With the food there
is no problem; we have long learned the basic
methods of wrapping foods to preserve them. But
what do you do about leftover wines?

There are some common sense rules which stem
from the fact that wine changes for the worse after
being open several hours. The two factors responsible
for that change are air and heat. Thus, partially
filled bottles should be tightly closed, either with
their own corks or with air-tight all-purpose
closures. This will prevent the entry of any new
air into the bottle and slow down the oxidation of
the wine. Then the bottles should be stored in the
refrigerator—both reds and whites (and Rosés) alike.
Numbed by the cold, the wine will remain stable for
a longer period than if exposed to the constant rise
and fall of temperatures of an ordinary room. (Even
leftover wine should be served at the proper
temperature. Remove the reds from the refrigerator
an hour before serving and uncork them. The whites
and Rosés may remain chilled until about fifteen
minutes before use, and they, too, should be
uncorked a few minutes before serving.)

Handled with care, wines which you enjoyed at a
special occasion on Saturday evening will be
palatable and enjoyable the following Wednesday,

Thursday, or even Friday. And wise homemakers will find them excellent for cooking even after a week.

Serving and Rebottling "Jug" Wines. Once you've become a wine buff, you'll probably find yourself investing in the gallon jugs of reds, whites, and Rosés that offer excellent drinking at a moderate price. They have the ability to lift an ordinary meal to the status of a feast — and, literally, for just pennies!

But unless the wine-drinking population of your family numbers at least four, you may have a problem keeping the wine good after the gallon jug has been opened. Since the screw caps on these jugs offer an excellent seal, there will be little problem in keeping them up to a week, but should your gallon promise to stretch longer than that, by all means *rebottle the wine.* This may sound like a formidable process, but it's really quite simple. Save some old fifth bottles with their corks. When the time comes to use them, sterilize them in boiling water — a large baby-bottle sterilizer is ideal for this purpose. Pour the wine from the gallon jug into the freshly sterilized fifth bottles to within an inch of the top — the less air space the better — and close with a cork. Thus rebottled, the wine should keep in the refrigerator for weeks. (Of course, any bottle stoppered with a cork should be laid on its side to keep the cork from drying and admitting air.)

KEEPING AND STORING WINE

> *"I love everything that's old: old friends, old times, old manners, old books, old wine."*
>
> —*Oliver Goldsmith*

The Home Wine "Cellar"

The phrase "wine cellar" is romantic, calling up visions of picturesque stone caves with cobwebs in the corners and lichen on the roof, lined with bottles of rare vintage. It is also intimidating if you don't happen to own the kind of mansion that usually goes with such a cellar. Many modern homes don't even have basements, and a large segment of Americans live in apartments.

If lack of your very own subterranean cave has kept you from the enjoyment of collecting wines, it shouldn't have, and needn't any longer. You don't need a genuine cellar to have a wine cellar. Good wine cellars may be located in all sorts of unlikely places—broom closets, kitchen cabinets, even under the sink. Even if your home does happen to have a cellar, it may not be suitable for wine. Such existing tenants as the furnace, the washer, and the dryer do not make good roommates for wine, since between the heat of the furnace and the vibration of the appliances, the wine is likely to come out a poor loser.

Heat is the worst enemy of wine. Ideally, a wine cellar should not be too hot or too cold (although white wines and Champagnes keep nicely in a refrigerator), not too damp (the labels turn moldy

301

and disintegrate), and not too dry (the corks dry out). Fifty to 60° F. is the temperature range in which wine thrives. A somewhat higher temperature may cause your wine to age too quickly and less smoothly. Should the temperature rise much above 70° F. there may be seepage of the wine through the cork — in which case you should drink it at once.

Equally important to a wine's well-being is stability. Great variations in temperature — 45° F. at night, 60° F. during the day, for example — are worse than a steady 65° F. Stability also applies to movement. Wine thrives in a restful environment. Thus it should be kept far from vibrating appliances — washers, dryers, elevator shafts. In fact, wine thrives best in peaceful, cool darkness. Light, and particularly sunlight, is damaging. The use of dark glass for wine bottles is more than just a tradition; it is the age-old method of shielding wine from light.

So if you are lucky enough to have a stone cellar, select a dark corner well away from the furnace room. But if heavy appliances are frequently at work, try an ordinary closet above ground.

An interior closet should be your first choice, since it is far more likely to have an even temperature than an outside wall exposed to the comings and goings of the sun. (If you must settle upon an outside closet, remember that the wall that faces the afternoon sun will probably get warmer and be more subject to temperature changes than the other three.)

The floor of a closet is generally several degrees cooler than a high shelf, but should you have any doubts, it might be helpful to test the temperature range with a household thermometer. If none of your closets measure up, you might try lining the most promising with insulating board.

Wine Racks

Wine is generally stored with the bottles resting on their sides so that the corks won't dry out and admit air. Corked bottles, in addition to being stored flat, are usually placed with their necks forward so that you can spot any leaking bottles and use them immediately. Wine racks for corked bottles may be as elaborate or as simple as you choose. Attractive wooden or metal racks come in sizes for twelve, twenty-four, fifty, or even a hundred bottles, and are obtainable in most furniture and department stores.

However, these handsomely designed racks are really pieces of furniture. They're meant to be seen, not to be hidden away in your closet wine cellar. So if you want to show off some of your collection — without risk of spoiling the wines — it's wise to get one of the smaller racks to hold just the wines you intend using right away. (You needn't fill *every* slot — a few empty ones make it look used.) The balance of your "cellar" can remain in the cool darkness to which it is accustomed and in which it thrives best.

As for the collection itself, you may prefer to spend your money on wine rather than wine racks. There are many everyday objects that can be turned into quite suitable wine racks. The simplest and least expensive is a fiberboard case box, which your local dealer will be quite happy to let you have. Laid flat on its side, with the dividers left in, it will hold twelve bottles — and several boxes can be stacked one atop another, to provide an instant rack at no cost. However, for handy collectors, the vinyl self-sticking decorative paper is a boon; use it to cover the case boxes for an individualized wine "rack" you can display whenever you feel the need to show off.

Another quickly assembled "rack" can be made from big, 46-ounce fruit juice cans with one or both ends cut off. Lay them in rows on the closet floor or shelf. The only carpentry required may be some kind of vertical brace at each end of the rows to keep the cans from rolling. (Or you can glue the cans together with epoxy cement.)

Agricultural tile is a similar approach, but slightly more expensive. It does have the advantage of insulating where air temperature tends to fluctuate more than you think wise. Wine bottles fit inside the 4-inch diameter tiles.

And, of course, for those handy with tools, there are the do-it-yourself racks. Here are three basic designs you can adapt to your own storage space.

Once your racks are installed, you have only to place the wine – in layers, according to type. An easy rule to follow is to store the wine according to how you would serve it. Sparkling wines are served icy cold; they belong on the bottom layer where it is coolest. White wines are produced in cool conditions and are served chilled. They come next, followed by the Rosés, and then the reds, which are fermented at higher temperatures and served at cool room temperature.

Because appetizer and dessert wines have become acclimated to a certain degree of warmth – both in the growing and winemaking stages – they are the last to suffer from higher temperatures and may be safely stored on the top shelf of your "cellar." In fact, it's a good idea to put some of them on the top shelf and forget about them for it's impossible to store some of them – Madeira, Marsala, Cream Sherry – too long.

Stocking Your Cellar

If you are a beginner, you may be wondering which wines to begin with. Perhaps the simplest way to start is with a case or two of assorted wines: some appetizer wines – Dry Vermouth and Cocktail Sherry; a dessert wine such as Port or Cream Sherry; for festive occasions, a bottle or two of Champagne – one Extra Dry for before or after dinner, another – Brut – to go with the food. You may wish to include a bottle of Sparkling Burgundy for less formal occasions. White wines, whether imported or American, do not improve with age and some actually start downhill a few years after leaving the winery, so stock white wines more or less as you intend to use them – perhaps a month's supply. For your "starter cellar" you may want to try one of each of the following: a Pinot Chardonnay, a Chenin Blanc, a Sauvignon Blanc, a Riesling, a Catawba, a Delaware.

Like the whites, Rosés do not improve with age. Meant to be drunk young, they remain virtually the same from the day they are bottled. Two bottles should be enough to start with, unless you're a Rosé devotée – and there are many! Experiment with the Grenache Rosé, the Gamay Rosé and the Zinfandel Rosé; each has the distinctive flavor and robustness of its particular grape.

Among the reds, Gamay (also Gamay Beaujolais) and Chianti are not worth aging. These light, fruity wines are also meant to be drunk young; when you buy one of them, it is as interesting as it ever will be. A bottle or two should do for your cellar to start.

But the noble Cabernet Sauvignons and Pinot Noirs (as with France's Bordeaux and Burgundies) are wines you will want to keep. When you find one you particularly like, buy a few bottles to lay away. ("Put down" is another phrase to describe the loving storage of a particular favorite—despite its derogatory meaning in contemporary slang.) Each year you keep these wines they will be improving—growing into wines with very different characters than they had when you bought them. (An economic note: Fine red wines not only get better with age, they become more valuable. It is not unusual for a bottle of wine to triple in value in a decade.) And while on the subject of red wines, do not overlook the Zinfandels. Possessed of some of the best characteristics of the Cabernets, these wines, though good when young, can become great with four or five years of age.

Storing "Jug" Wines

By all means, keep room in your cellar for the everyday wines—the economical jug wines which are not meant for aging but which nevertheless make very good drinking! With no cork to keep dry, these screw-top bottles may be stored upright and will retain the quality of the wine for at least a year.

There's your wine "cellar"—or at least its start! This basic collection is the kind most of us have. It guarantees us a choice of wines for every occasion as well as the beginning knowledge for a wonderful hobby.

Later, if the collecting bug bites, you may want to expand, stocking other favorites as you discover them. However large your collection becomes, you'll find the same rules apply.

MAKE YOUR NEXT PARTY A WINE TASTING!

"If food is the body of good living, wine is its soul."
—Clifton Fadiman

As interest in wine grows, more and more people want to know more and more about it, which has led to the popularity of the wine tasting party. This new way of entertaining has all the elements of success. It brings together congenial people and gives them something to talk about because wine is such a complex beverage, it is something to be discussed; it stimulates "ice-breaking" conversation, thus relieving the busy host and hostess of a potential major headache.

There are many different kinds of tastings. If your guests are newcomers to wine, you may want to introduce them to the widest range of wine types, letting them discover the ones they like best. The appetizer wines might include a cocktail Sherry and some sweet and dry Vermouths; among the table wines, a Burgundy and/or Claret, a Rosé, a pink Catawba, and—in the whites—a Riesling, Elvira, and Chablis. Port and Muscatel make a good contrast in the dessert wine category. Just for comparison, you may want to include a European wine in each of the categories—and you may just be surprised at the preference for the American vintages!

This kind of tasting is the most basic, really an introduction to the various wine types. A more sophisticated group would enjoy a tasting limited to table wines, or to all reds or all whites. You might have two or more brands of each type and take a vote at the end of the evening to determine the most popular.

Still another tasting could focus on varietal wines—all red or all white, compared with generic wines of the same type. The possibilities are limitless, as you can see in the following wine-tasting lists:

Red Wine Tasting

Claret
Zinfandel
Cabernet Sauvignon
Gamay Beaujolais
Burgundy
Pinot Noir

White Wine Tasting

Emerald Riesling
Johannisburg Riesling
Elvira
Chablis
Pinot Chardonnay
Sauvignon Blanc
Haut (or Château) Sauterne

Rosés

Catawba
Vin Rosé
Gamay Rosé
Napa Rosé
Grenache Rosé

In each of these categories, the lighter wines have been listed first—and they are the ones to be tasted first. Then go to the fuller-bodied wines for comparison.

Games add fun to any wine tasting and let your

guests test their new-found expertise. Blindfold the contestants and set before each a glass of red, white, and Rosé wine—all at room temperature. From smell and taste alone, let them determine which is which. It's not as easy as it sounds!

Then try a *triangular tasting*. This also involves three glasses of wine per player: two containing the same wine, the third a different, but similar wine— perhaps a Burgundy to compare with two different Pinot Noirs. Since the wines will look the same, no blindfold is needed. Let the contestant decide which two glasses are the same. And to lengthen the odds against a lucky guess, have the players do the test twice!

A test for comparative *sweetness* is ideal for Champagnes. Choose a *Brut*—the driest of all, and a *Sec*—slightly sweeter. Cover the labels and any other identification, and pour a glass of each type (number the glasses to avoid confusion). Let the contestant's taste buds identify the wine.

The above are just a few of the games that can develop from a wine tasting; the more you learn about different wines, the more complicated your tests can become.

Giving a wine tasting party is one of the easiest ways to entertain. Nevertheless, it does take some planning. First, decide how much wine you will need. The more types you taste, the more bottles are required—thus the wisdom of a limited tasting. You must allow about two ounces of each different wine for each guest. Since the fifth bottle contains 25.6 ounces, you may figure twelve tastes to the bottle.

(It's a good idea to keep one extra bottle of each wine in reserve, for those who come back for seconds of their favorite.)

You will need glasses, preferably stemmed glasses designed for wine service. Since your own stemware collection isn't likely to stretch to twenty-five (an average tasting), you will find any number of rental services eager to supply your needs at minimum cost. In any case, you do not need a glass for every wine for every guest. Professional wine tasters are quite accustomed to rinsing out their glasses after each taste from a pitcher of water provided by you. The water is then poured into a bowl, which should be emptied at regular intervals. Thus, the same glass serves for each wine. (For very large groups, however, you may find those clear, plastic, disposable glasses a convenient and inexpensive substitute.)

Food for a wine tasting can be as elaborate or as simple as you wish. The traditional tasting is usually limited to bread — a small bite eaten to cleanse the palate between tastes of different wines — and, perhaps, some mild cheese. However, any kind of canapés — cocktail franks, baby shrimp, finger foods, tidbits that can be eaten from a toothpick — are easiest for both you and your guests, and are appropriate, along with some nuts and fruits to go with the dessert wines, if you include them in the tasting. Just be sure that the food is not so pungent as to overwhelm the flavor of the wines. Blue cheese, for example, while it goes well with wine for drinking, is much too strong for a tasting of two ounces of beverage. The milder Port Saluts and Muensters are a much better choice — satisfying without being devastating to the wine.

Be sure you have a workable corkscrew on hand; remember to chill the white wines and Rosés for a few hours; and open all the wines an hour or so before serving. And that's all there is to a wine tasting!

These are the basics; and they remain the same whether the tasting is a small gathering at your home, a community social for 100, or a giant fund-raising event for 1000.

However, for large groups, some additional preliminary planning is in order. Consider first the wines. American tastes vary from sweet to completely dry and, since you'll want to please as many as you can, you should probably include appetizer and dessert wines in your list. Don't try to be more sophisticated than your audience. And in the table wines, which tend to be dry, be sure to include some for those who prefer the softer, more mellow vintages: among the reds, a Vino Rosso; in the whites, a sweet Sauvignon Blanc, a white Catawba, a Niagara, or semi-sweet Delaware, an Haut Sauterne. In the Rosés, be sure to list a pink Catawba. And the dessert wines should include at least one of the rich, sweet, fruity Concords.

A large tasting also demands organization of labor. There should be a committee for glasses — responsible for rental, or buying of suitable substitutes (if you are using the plastic cups, you should have one for each wine, and since they are inexpensive there should be no problem). If the budget is especially tight, French bread broken into bite-size pieces and small, unsalted crackers will do; if you have more to spend, cubes of American cheese will provide an extra enjoyment. With a large group, never try to be exotic; your efforts will go unnoticed. Instead, supplement the wine with constructive ways and means for the taster to obtain the most pleasure.

Wine lists are very important. A literature committee should mimeograph a list of the wines — brands and types, with spaces provided for guests to write comments. If possible, you may want to expand your list to include classic descriptions of the wines to be tasted — along with the foods they are traditionally served with.

WINE AND HEALTH

"Wine is the most healthful and hygienic of all beverages."
— *Louis Pasteur*

Remember the lesson in school health classes: drink
eight glasses of water a day, *but not with meals?* We
were told that in some mysterious way all that water
was good for us all day long — but not while we ate!
Well, there is a reason; water dilutes the stomach
juices that digest food. No such warning was
necessary in Europe where, for centuries, wine has
been drunk with meals. Certain acidic elements in
wine so closely resemble those of the gastric juices
that dry table wine has been found to be an actual
aid to digestion.

In fact, wine is one of those wonderful, rare things
in life that is not only good, but good for you!
Because wine is actually a food — the result of
natural fermenting of natural foods — it is a source
of nourishment. And while no chemical analysis has
ever completely defined the composition of wine, it is
known to contain valuable vitamins — including
significant amounts of the B-vitamins, as well as
such minerals as calcium and iron. (With little or no
guidance, except their own taste, Europeans seem to
have sensed the "secret" of wine long before it came
to the attention of the medical fraternity. They
drank it — and still do — because it makes good food
taste even better. But they also used wine to build
up anemic blood, to awaken a poor appetite, to
supply energy to the lethargic on one hand, and to
calm the nerves of the hyperactive on the other.)

313

Wine has long been a staple in the ordinary convalescent diet in European hospitals. Just imagine the outrage of a Frenchman laid low with a mere broken leg — yet denied his quarter-litre of wine with dinner! But only fairly recently have American hospitals begun experimenting with wine. The results of these experiments have been more than just of passing interest.

Naturally, wine is offered a patient only with permission of the presiding physician. Obviously, such conditions as liver or kidney diseases, or any trace of an alcoholic problem would rule it out. However, in those cases where wine was not contraindicated, the addition of dry table wine has had a significant effect on the convalescent process. Patients' rating of hospital food soared astronomically when wine became part of the meal; even the coffee — long the bane of the patient-victim — tasted better. In addition, hospital noises, uncomfortable beds, and other perennial complaints of the hospitalized were reduced.

Much of wine's benefit can be attributed to its tranquilizing effect. Not only does it act as a mild sedative; it has the effect of reaffirming to the patient his place in the human race. For this reason, it is considered to be a socio-psychological as well as medical treatment, especially in gerentology,

314

the care of elderly patients who all too often feel themselves cut off from the mainstream of life. As one doctor put it, "There's a big difference between ordering an old man to take his medicine, and offering him a drink."

Though wine is probably the oldest medicine in the world — and one that has been in constant use throughout history — new benefits are constantly being discovered. For example, it has been found that wine, in some mysterious way, helps to combat the build-up of cholesterol. In comparative studies, the rate of heart disease was found significantly lower in European countries where wine is the usual accompaniment to a meal than in American families of comparable wealth and status. Closer to home is the case of the small Pennsylvania town of Roseto, an Italian-American community where wine is part of daily life and heart disease is remarkably lower than in any other part of the country.

Doctors, therefore, are allowing more and more of their heart patients wine with their meals — it has the added advantage of brightening up the otherwise rigid diet. Dry table wines are also permitted on diabetic diets (their alcohol is metabolized without insulin) and even recovering ulcer patients — to whom stronger drinks are forbidden — are offered a relaxing glass of wine to supplement their otherwise bland diets.

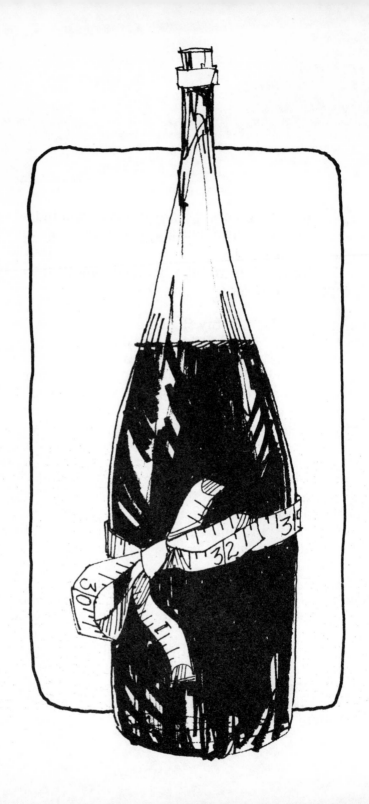

DIETING WITH WINE

"A man who was fond of wine was offered some grapes at dessert after dinner. 'Much obliged,' he said, pushing the plate aside. 'I'm not accustomed to taking my wine in pills.'"
— *Anthelme Brillat-Savarin*

The best wine news of all is for dieters! The fad diet, whether low-carbohydrate or low-calorie, can include dry table wine because it contains only a "trace" of carbohydrates and is lower in calories than other alcoholic drink except beer — about 90 calories for an average serving of four ounces.

The wine label tells the calories along with the alcoholic content. Just double that figure to get the approximate calories per ounce. Most dry wines are 12 percent to 14 percent alcohol — 24 to 28 calories to the ounce. (Compare that with the figures for whiskey, gin, and other distilled alcohols where "proof" actually equals the calories. One-hundred proof vodka is 100 calories per ounce.) The average serving of red table wine is four ounces — around 96 calories — which will fit into any diet. And if you really want to scrimp, the white wines are about five or six calories less per drink.

Wine with the meal not only makes everything taste better, it's been found that wine dieters have less craving for fattening, starchy foods — they limit their carbohydrate intake naturally and painlessly.

Of course, if you are dieting under a doctor's supervision, you should check with him before including wine. But I've yet to find a physician who'd say "no" to wine — so long as the daily calorie count wasn't exceeded.

317

STRAWBERRIES IN WINE

1 pound strawberries
1 cup red wine
1 teaspoon low-calorie sweetener

Prepare well-ripened strawberries — remove the
stems, wash, dry. Mix the sweetener with the wine.
Pour it over the strawberries. Moisten them several
times before putting them in the refrigerator. Chill
for at least an hour before serving. (75 calories per
portion) *Serves 4.*

ICED MELON

4 small ripe cantaloupes
1 cup Port

Cut off the tops near to the stem, and put them
aside. Carefully remove the seeds with a spoon. If
the melon does not stand up well, slice away the
bottom just a little to give the melon more stability.
Pour 2 ounces of Port into each melon. Replace the
tops. Put in the refrigerator for several hours. Serve
well chilled. (135 calories per portion) *Serves 4.*

CHICKEN IN WINE

1 young chicken, about 2 pounds
½ cup Brandy
1 onion, sliced
2 garlic cloves, mashed
1 pound small fresh mushrooms, washed but
  not peeled
1 tablespoon flour
1 cup red wine
Salt and pepper

Cut chicken in pieces. Put in heavy pot over high
heat. As pieces begin to brown, warm Brandy in
small saucepan and pour over chicken. Ignite. Add
onions, garlic and mushrooms. Sprinkle with flour.
Add wine, little by little. Salt and pepper to taste.
Cover tightly and simmer gently for 1 hour. (300
calories per portion) *Serves 4.*

SCALLOPS IN WHITE WINE

¾ lb scallops (if large sea scallops, cut in
  quarters)
½ cup white wine
2 onions, chopped
1 clove garlic, minced
Salt and pepper
2 tablespoons cracker crumbs
2 tablespoons chopped parsley

Pour wine into small baking dish and add scallops.
Cover with onions and garlic. Sprinkle with salt,
pepper, and cracker crumbs. Bake in (350° F.)
oven for 15 minutes. Garnish with chopped parsley
and serve immediately. (100 calories per portion)
Serves 2.

HAM AND CABBAGE

1 lean, raw ham slice of about 1 pound
2 cups dry white wine
2 cups water
2 medium onions, quartered
2 carrots cut into inch pieces
$\frac{1}{4}$ teaspoon dill seed
$\frac{1}{4}$ teaspoon thyme
$\frac{1}{4}$ teaspoon peppercorns
Salt
1 head cabbage (about 2 pounds), cut in wedges

Soak ham overnight in fresh water. Remove the fat.
Place in a bouillon of wine and water, onion, carrots
and peppercorns. Cook for about 2 hours. 20
minutes before it is done, add the cabbage; drain
before serving. (310 calories per portion) *Serves 4.*

MEDITERRANEAN SOLE

2 medium tomatoes, peeled, seeded, and chopped
4 medium mushrooms, chopped
2 tablespoons finely chopped shallots
2 tablespoons chopped parsley
2 sole fillets, 5 ounces each
$\frac{1}{2}$ cup dry white wine
Salt and pepper

Spread half the tomatoes in a baking dish. Sprinkle
with half the chopped mushrooms, shallots, and
parsley. Add fish and cover with rest of the tomatoes,
shallots, mushrooms and parsley. Pour over white
wine, sprinkle lightly with salt and pepper, and
bake in a moderate (350° F.) oven for about 30
minutes. (145 calories per portion) *Serves 2.*

LOW-CALORIE BEEF BURGUNDY

1½ pound lean chuck beef
1 teaspoon salad oil
1 medium onion, sliced
1 tablespoon flour
1 cup red wine
Pinches of salt, pepper, thyme, parsley, oregano
1 bay leaf
4 ounces mushrooms

Cut the beef into 1-inch cubes. Heat oil in a pot, brown the sliced onions, then the meat. Sprinkle with flour and stir for 3 or 4 minutes more before adding the wine and water. Then add the salt, pepper, thyme, bay leaf, parsley, oregano. Allow to simmer over low heat not more than 3 hours. Fifteen minutes before serving, add the mushrooms. (370 calories per portion) *Serves 4.*

BEEF CURRY

1 teaspoon salad oil
1 pound fresh onions, thinly sliced
1 tablespoon flour
¾ cup water
⅓ cup white wine
Salt and pepper
1 tablespoon curry powder (or more, according to taste)

Heat the oil in a pot. When well heated, brown the onions. Sprinkle them with flour without allowing any lumps to form. Add water, wine, salt, pepper, curry.
Add beef to pot and allow to simmer for 1½ hours over low heat. Cover well. Uncover a few minutes before serving if there is too much liquid. (335 calories per portion) *Serves 4.*

LAMB VERMOUTH

1½ pounds lean, boneless lamb shoulder
4 tablespoons lemon juice
2 garlic cloves, mashed
2 onions chopped
1 teaspoon curry powder
Salt and pepper
2 cups water
½ cup dry vermouth

Sprinkle lamb with lemon juice. Place in an oven
dish. Add the garlic, onion, curry, salt and pepper.
Put in a hot (450°) oven for ½ hour; add the water,
basting often. Add vermouth and lower heat to 350° F.
Bake in oven for ¼ hour more. Serve very hot.
(350 calories per portion) *Serves 4.*

TOMATO-BEEF PATTIES

4 ounces peeled tomatoes
1 garlic clove, chopped
1 teaspoon chopped onion
1 tablespoon chopped parsley
2 tablespoons white wine
Salt and pepper
½ pound ground beef, formed into patties

Put tomatoes in a small saucepan. Sprinkle with
garlic, onions and parsley. Add the white wine, salt,
pepper and allow to reduce for 20 minutes, over a
low fire. Add the beef patties. Cover pan well and
cook for 8 to 10 minutes. (260 calories per portion)
Serves 2.

322

MEAT PATTIES BURGUNDY

½ pound chopped lean beef
½ pound chopped lean veal
2 small onions, chopped
2 whole eggs
4 tablespoons chopped parsley
Salt and pepper
1 cup Burgundy
2 tomatoes, sliced
4 ounces mushrooms

Mix meats with onions, eggs and ⅔ of the parsley.
Salt and pepper. Divide the preparation into 8 equal
parts and shape patties into oblongs. Pour half the
wine into a small oven dish. Place the patties in the
dish, tomato slices on top. Sprinkle with remaining
parsley. Surround with the mushrooms. Pour on
remaining wine. Serve very hot after baking for a
half-hour in a moderate (350° F.) oven. (350 calories
per portion) *Serves 4.*

INDEX